PYRAMIDS & TOMBS OF
ANCIENT EGYPT

PYRAMIDS & TOMBS OF
ANCIENT EGYPT

An illustrated   :ivilization

southwater

*For my husband John and all our
many friends in Egypt*

This edition is published by Southwater

Southwater is an imprint of
Anness Publishing Ltd, Hermes House,
88–89 Blackfriars Road, London SE1 8HA
tel. 020 7401 2077; fax 020 7633 9499
www.southwaterbooks.com
info@anness.com

© Anness Publishing Limited 2003

This edition distributed in the UK
by The Manning Partnership Ltd
tel. 01225 478 444; fax 01225 478 440
sales@manning-partnership.co.uk

This edition distributed in the USA
and Canada by National Book Network
tel. 301 459 3366; fax 301 429 5746
www.nbnbooks.com

This edition distributed in Australia
by Pan Macmillan Australia
tel. 1300 135 113; fax 1300 135 103
customer.service@macmillan.com.au

This edition distributed in New Zealand
by The Five Mile Press (NZ) Ltd
tel. (09) 444 4144; fax (09) 444 4518
fivemilenz@xtra.co.nz

Publisher: Joanna Lorenz
Managing Editor: Linda Fraser
Project Editor: Laura Seber
Designer: Jez MacBean
Jacket Designer: Balley Design
Illustrator: Chris Orr
Production Controller: Darren Price
Editorial Reader: Penelope Goodare

1 2 3 4 5 6 7 8 9 10

*Page 1 A detail from the so-called coronation chair
of Tutankhamun; Page 2 The majestic Sphinx before
the pyramid of Khafre at Giza; Page 3 Queen Tuya's
jewel box from the tomb she shared with her husband,
Yuya; Page 4 The goddess Hathor welcomes Seti I
into the Afterlife; Page 5 A statue of Amenemhet III
from his pyramid complex at Hawara*

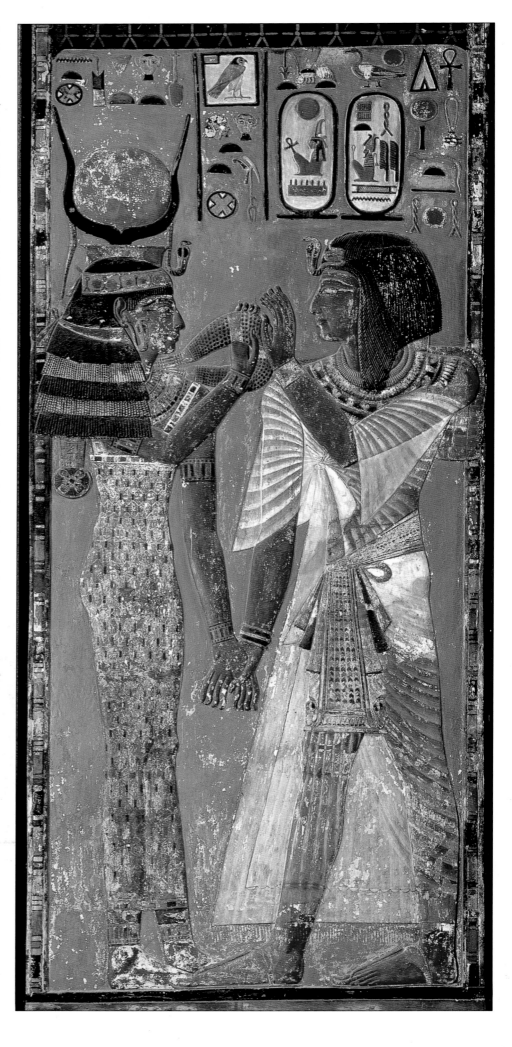

CONTENTS

Introduction: Ancient Egypt in Context 6

The Rediscovery of Ancient Egypt 8

The Development of the Pyramid Complex 28

The Pyramids of Giza 48

Memphis and Saqqara 70

The Valley of the Kings 90

Queens, Princes and Officials 110

Index 126

Acknowledgements 128

Ancient Egypt in Context

The fourth millennium BC was a time of great importance to the ancient Egyptians. It was the main formative period, when the individual cultures of different areas were gradually replaced by that of Naqada, an important Predynastic centre in the south. The archaeological record has revealed the spread of the culture known as Naqada II, characterized by attractive buff-coloured pottery decorated with lively scenes of ships, animals and dancing women, throughout the Nile Valley and the Delta.

Political centralization seems to have followed in the wake of cultural unity and is encapsulated in the Narmer Palette, a famous ceremonial object now in the Cairo Museum, which was found at Hierakonpolis, another great, early southern centre. This depicts the early king Narmer (c.3100 BC), wearing the crown of Upper Egypt, subduing people of the Delta, and shows him a second time wearing the crown of Lower Egypt. The point at which unification took place is still a matter of discussion, although it is now thought that the Narmer Palette reflects an established situation, with a sole king already in control of the 'Two Lands', rather than recording the conquest of the north by a southern king, as was once proposed. Ongoing excavations at Abydos have brought to light the graves of kings of the Predynastic Period, who are now referred to as Dynasty Zero. Signs scratched on labels once attached to the grave goods of these rulers also attest to the development of writing at an earlier period than was previously thought.

From c.3100 BC, there is evidence for the existence of a capital city at Memphis. Finds from the related cemetery sites of Saqqara and Abydos show that at this time Egypt enjoyed a high level of artistic achievement, was engaged in far-flung trading relations and was administered by a highly organized and structured bureaucracy.

Although little is known of political events during the Old Kingdom (c.2686–c.2181 BC) which followed, the period is famous for its monumental architecture. The pyramids of Giza are testimony to the status of the kings and their control over resources of materials and labour, and not least the ability of the administration to organize such colossal enterprises.

This period of strength was followed by well over a century of insecurity, when the rule of Egypt was divided during the First Intermediate Period (c.2181–c.2055 BC). However, towards 2000 BC the kings who ruled from Thebes managed to establish control over the whole country. Mentuhotep II (c.2055–c.2004 BC), who reunited Egypt at the

▼ *During the 4th Dynasty, the kings of Egypt were buried in the famous pyramids at Giza in northern Egypt.*

beginning of the Middle Kingdom (c.2055–c.1650 BC), was always regarded with great reverence by later kings. In spite of the fact that Amenemhat I (c.1985–c.1955 BC) may have been a usurper and was probably assassinated, the Twelfth Dynasty kings were strong rulers who established control not only over the whole of Egypt but also over Nubia, where several fortresses near the Second Cataract were built to protect Egyptian trading interests.

The ensuing Second Intermediate Period (c.1650–c.1550 BC) was again a time of divided rule. The Hyksos kings, probably originating in the Syria–Palestine area, took over the Nile Delta, and the rule of the Egyptian kings was confined to the south. The texts known as The Story of Seqenenre and Apepi, as well as the Kamose Stela erected in the Temple of Amun at Karnak, tell of the attempts of the Egyptian kings to drive out the Hyksos, while the autobiography of Ahmose (a soldier in the army of King Ahmose) records their eventual success.

Many of the sites visited by tourists today belong to the New Kingdom (c.1550–c.1069 BC). The temples of Luxor and Karnak, the mortuary temples of the West Bank and the royal tombs of the Valley of the Kings are witness to the power and prosperity of Egypt at this time, as are the Tombs of the Nobles, the final resting places of the officials who served the kings of the Eighteenth, Nineteenth and Twentieth Dynasties. During this period, Egypt also controlled many of the petty states of Syria–Palestine and Nubia.

However, from the end of the Twentieth Dynasty, Egypt entered a period of comparative weakness, when the kings ruled the north and the high priests of Amun at Karnak ruled the south, although relations between the two seem to have been friendly. Egypt appears to have lost her former status in Syria–Palestine, while Nubia became independent, with a Kushite ruling family based in the city of Napata in the Sudan, to the south of the Fourth Cataract. These Kushite kings invaded Egypt in the mid-eighth century BC, and were later acknowledged as the Twenty-fifth Dynasty. In 701 BC, the Kushite king, Taharqo (690–664 BC), went to the aid of King Hezekiah of Jerusalem, who was threatened by Sennacherib of Assyria. Taharqo's temerity in supporting a rebellious vassal provoked Assyrian

▲ In the New Kingdom, the royal tombs were situated in southern Egypt, in the remote area now known as the Valley of the Kings.

wrath: Egypt was subdued and became part of the Assyrian Empire for a time during the reign of Sennacherib's grandson, Ashurbanipal.

The governors of the Delta city of Sais at first ruled with Assyrian backing but were later to reign as the independent kings of the Twenty-sixth Dynasty. The Saite Period (664–525 BC) is regarded as an era of renaissance: culturally, there was a great deal of interest in the art and architecture of the past, which was consciously copied, but the period was also marked by a new realism in both sculpture and literature. Egypt was once again a united country under a firm central authority and became a power to be reckoned with on the world stage. Military campaigns were mounted to regain control of Nubia, and the Greek historian, Herodotus, describes an expedition sent by Nekau II (610–595 BC) to circumnavigate Africa.

Thereafter, the history of ancient Egypt is one of conquest by foreign powers: the Persians, Alexander the Great and finally Rome. ◆

The Rediscovery of Ancient Egypt

Egypt has always been a source of fascination for the traveller. The romantic landscape of the River Nile, with its magnificent antiquities set among the palms of the fertile valley, and the allure of the barren desert stretching away to the horizon never fail to capture the hearts and minds of visitors. But one visit is never enough. The first acquaintance makes such an impact that we are left totally speechless with wonder. With the second and third visits we start to believe our eyes, and the great antiquity and achievements of this ancient civilization begin to sink in. Add to this the charm of the people, their friendliness and unfailing good humour, courtesy and hospitality, and we are permanently hooked.

From the time of Herodotus onwards, Greek and Roman visitors to Egypt were fascinated by the pyramids and the Valley of the Kings. European interest was awakened in the seventeenth century, when the first attempts were made to record the monuments. This eventually led to rivalry between European nations and the race began to build up the Egyptian collections in the great museums of the world.

◀ *A watercolour painted in 1923 by Douglas Macpherson shows a statue of Tutankhamun guarding the entrance to his burial chamber, which was entirely filled by a nest of four gilded wooden shrines placed over the sarcophagus.*

Early Travellers to Egypt

The earliest traveller known to have fallen under the spell of Egypt was the Greek historian Herodotus (c.490–c.420 BC). He visited Egypt in the mid-fifth century BC, and later recorded his travels in Book Two of his great work *The Histories*. This work is primarily about the war between Greece and Persia in the earlier part of that century, but it is much more than a blow-by-blow account of events. Herodotus is often called the 'Father of History' because of his breadth of vision and the far-ranging scope of his work. He was interested in the deep-rooted causes of the war, the previous history of the powers involved, and the achievements and customs of their peoples. Because Egypt was part of the Persian Empire at the time of the war, he included a section on Egypt. Nobody had ever written anything like it before.

The travels of Herodotus

Concerning his trip to Egypt, Herodotus wrote: 'I went and saw for myself as far as Elephantine, but further information is from hearsay'. The truth of his account is sometimes doubted. Writing about the building of the Giza pyramids, for instance, he was referring to a period 2,000 years before his own time, and he had to rely on what he was told by the Egyptian priests. He often provided two or more versions of an event, leaving his readers to make up their own minds. However, on the history of the Twenty-sixth Dynasty (664–525 BC), he is the best ancient source. Modern archaeology continues to prove that much of what he said about this period was true.

Strabo

The Greek historian and geographer Strabo (c.63 BC–c.AD 21) spent several years in Alexandria, the capital planned by Alexander the Great, though he did not live to see it built, on the Mediterranean coast. It was extended and embellished with additional buildings by the Ptolemies, who ruled Egypt after him. Strabo's description is one of the main sources of information about it:

The city has magnificent public precincts and royal palaces, which cover a fourth or even a third of the entire area. For just as each of the kings would from a love of splendour add some ornament to the public monuments, so he would provide himself at his own expense with a residence in addition to those already standing.

Alexandria's public buildings included the great Museum, with its covered walk and dining hall for the convenience of scholars studying at the nearby Library. The two harbours and the lighthouse are also mentioned by Strabo, as well as the Theatre, the Gymnasium and the Temple of Serapis.

The whole city was criss-crossed with streets at right angles to each other, wide enough to take large numbers of horses and carriages. Strabo's description is particularly useful because much of the ancient city has disappeared under later building or now lies below the sea. It is exceptionally valuable to the teams of modern archaeologists who are now bringing parts of the old city to light.

Strabo also visited Upper Egypt, and described the tourist attractions of the day, such as the Colossi of Memnon and the royal tombs in the Valley of the Kings. About the latter he wrote: 'Above the Memnonium [the Ramesseum], are the tombs of the kings, which are hewn in stone, are about 40 in number, are marvellously constructed, and a spectacle worth seeing'.

▼ *At his Tivoli residence, Hadrian encapsulated the places and works of art he had seen on his travels in Greece and Egypt.*

▲ *Although recent excavation has revealed more of the site, the two gigantic statues of Amenhotep III are all the tourist usually gets to see of this once enormous mortuary temple, which served the cult of the deceased king.*

The Colossi of Memnon

Strabo was rather scathing on the subject of these two massive statues, which represent Amenhotep III (c.1390–c.1352 BC) and mark the site of his once great funerary temple. In Strabo's day, however, they were identified with the mythical King Memnon of Ethiopia, said to be the son of the Dawn, a hero who had gone to the aid of the Trojans against the Greeks.

The statues had been damaged by an earthquake in 27 BC, and one of them was reputed to give out weird noises. Most tourists were greatly impressed and gathered daily to hear the statue speak. Strabo cynically put the mystery down to the machinations of the local priests.

Hadrian saw the same statue in AD 130, but it did not 'speak' until the second day of his visit. A poetess in the imperial retinue, Julia Balbilla, carved on the statue a verse in praise of Memnon and Hadrian. The inscription can still be read today.

Hadrian

When the Roman emperor Hadrian (AD 117–138) arrived in Egypt in AD 130, he went first to Alexandria. There he spent some time in learned discussions with the scholars in the Museum. He then sailed up the Nile accompanied by his favourite, Antinous, who was accidentally drowned during the trip. In memory of his friend,

▶ *Portrait bust of the Emperor Hadrian who spent much of his reign travelling around the Empire, visiting Greece in AD 125 and 128 and Egypt in AD 130.*

Hadrian founded a new city, Antinoopolis, which was laid out on a grid along Greek lines, with two colonnaded main streets crossing at right angles and embellished with baths, temples and a theatre.

Graffiti inscribed by the tourists of antiquity bear witness to the interest aroused by Egypt's buildings and monuments during the Roman Period. Paramount among these were the obelisks inscribed with hieroglyphs, which the Romans could not decipher. Several emperors had obelisks taken to Rome, where they still stand today. The Roman naturalist Pliny the Elder wrote that the Emperor Augustus (27 BC– AD 14) used the obelisk set up in the Campus Martius in Rome as a sort of

calendar, based on measurements of its shadow at various times throughout the year. Apparently it did not work. Emperor Constantine (AD 312–337) removed an obelisk of Tuthmosis III from its original site at Thebes and took it to Alexandria to await shipment to his new capital of Constantinople. Constantine died before the obelisk reached its destination, but Theodosius I finally set it up in the Hippodrome in AD 390.

Hadrian took an even more personal interest in the antiquities, and had some of them taken home to Italy to enhance his villa at Tivoli. It does not seem to be true, however, as scholars once thought, that he tried to recreate complete buildings. The building known today as the Serapaeum at Tivoli was once widely considered to be a 'replica' of the Temple of Serapis at Canopus near Alexandria, but is now identified as a triclinium (dining room). ◆

The Reawakening of European Interest

After the fall of the Roman Empire, Europe forgot about Egypt for a time. Egypt became a Muslim country, and it was in any case difficult for Europeans to travel beyond Cairo and the Nile Delta. During the Middle Ages, most interest was focused on Egypt's links – real or otherwise – with the Bible. The pyramids at Giza, for instance, were fancifully identified as 'Joseph's granaries'. For the most part, Egypt was merely a staging post on the well-worn pilgrim route to Jerusalem during this time. Any European interest in Egypt lay in its associations with early Christianity rather than in the land of the pharaohs.

Religious missions

It was only in the seventeenth century that European expeditions to Egypt began again, and these were undertaken mainly for religious reasons. Monks went to Cairo to preach the gospel, but some of them took the opportunity to travel further afield. In 1672, the Dominican priest Father Vansleb was instructed by Jean Baptiste Colbert, chief minister of Louis XIV of France, to collect coins and ancient manuscripts while in the country. He visited the Red and White Monasteries at Sohag and the Monastery of St Anthony on the Red Sea. He also took an interest in the antiquities, particularly the mummies. On opening a pit at Saqqara, he came upon a room full of mummified birds and took some examples back to Europe. Travelling further south, he was the first European to describe Antinoopolis.

Slightly later, between 1714 and 26, another French priest, Claude Sicard, went on to explore the rest of the country. Father Sicard was the leader of the first Jesuit mission to Cairo and eventually he drew up the first scientific map of Egypt. This showed the precise locations of Memphis and Thebes, and

▼ *An early 19th-century watercolour engraving by Louis François Cassas shows the Sphinx and the pyramid of Khafre at Giza.*

all the main temple sites. He also pinpointed ten open tombs in the Valley of the Kings.

Early descriptions

The best account to survive from this early period, however, was written by Richard Pococke, Bishop of Ossory in Ireland, who visited Egypt in the late 1730s. His description of the Valley of the Kings, where he found 18 tombs (although only nine were open), was published in 1743 under the title *Observations on Egypt*. He also produced a map of the Giza pyramids, but this is schematic in the extreme and his description of the site does not agree with what is found on the ground.

Pococke's contemporary, the Danish traveller Friderik Norden, also visited the pyramids. He was a naval marine architect, and in 1755 he published a much more accurate account than Pococke's in his *Travels in Egypt and Nubia*. He had been commissioned by King Christian VI of Denmark to collect information of antiquarian interest; he travelled the length of Egypt and eventually penetrated Nubia. Frustrated in his attempt to reach the Second Cataract, he got as far as Derr, where he wrote an account of the temple of Tuthmosis III (c.1479–1425 BC).

During his travels, Norden recorded a huge amount of information on the monuments of ancient Egypt. His book was widely read by scholars and laymen alike, and its importance in providing accurate plans and drawings cannot be exaggerated. He was also interested in contemporary life. He warned that the local people were suspicious of foreign travellers, being convinced that they were all treasure seekers and practitioners of black magic, and crowds gathered to see them. In order to allay any such suspicions, Norden advised prospective travellers not to try to touch the antiquities, but to adopt Turkish dress, 'a pair

of mustachios' and 'a grave and solemn air'. The first picture of a scene in a tomb in the Valley of the Kings was published in 1790 by the Scottish traveller, James Bruce. During his visit to the tomb of Ramesses III (c.1184–1153 BC) he was fascinated by a scene in a small side chamber, depicting harpists playing before some of the gods. Bruce's drawing is now lost but seems to have been elaborated by the plate-engraver who took many liberties with the

▲ *Richard Pococke's 'map' of the Valley of the Kings. Although not accurate in the modern sense, archaeologists have been able to identify the tombs Pococke visited from the accompanying plans.*

original. Having never seen any ancient Egyptian art, he interpreted it according to contemporary taste in the neo-classical style. Although his illustration of the harpists affords some amusement today, the tomb of Ramesses III has ever since been known as 'Bruce's tomb'. ◆

Napoleon's Expedition to Egypt

In 1798, Napoleon Bonaparte of France mounted a great expedition to Egypt with the dual purpose of reducing the power of his chief adversary, England, and exploring a lost civilization. His military expedition was a failure, but his survey of Egypt brought the wonders of the ancient land to the attention of the whole of Europe.

Before leaving for Egypt, Napoleon ordered leading French scholars to assemble teams of professional surveyors, engineers, mathematicians, astronomers, chemists and botanists, as well as artists, architects and archaeologists. These experts were to survey and record all aspects of Egyptian life, past and present. The French soon made themselves masters of Cairo, after defeating the Mameluke rulers, but were beaten at sea by Nelson's English fleet at the Battle of Abukir Bay. Finding themselves stranded in Egypt, the French Commission on Arts and Sciences spent the next three years mapping the whole country, recording archaeological sites and monuments, and studying the flora and fauna and contemporary life of the Egyptian people.

Description de l'Egypte

The result was a massive work, the *Description de l'Egypte,* published in 20 volumes between 1809 and 1828. This monumental, lavishly illustrated work caused a tremendous sensation among the scholars and cognoscenti of Europe, depicting as it did the splendours of ancient Egypt as they had never been seen before. The Commission's artists had drawn precise views of many of the pyramids. Khufu's Great Pyramid and the Sphinx had been carefully measured and studied.

Further south, the Commission explored the Valley of the Kings, where 16 tombs were located. The map of the valley, drawn for the expedition by Jollois and de Villiers, two young engineers, was the first accurate map of the area ever to be made. They also discovered a secondary valley, the Western Valley, and in it the tomb of Amenhotep III (c.1390–1352), whose existence had not previously been known.

▲ *Napoleon Bonaparte who, in 1798, mounted an expedition aimed at the conquest of Egypt. This was accompanied by a special commission that recorded the flora, fauna and contemporary culture of Egypt and surveyed the antiquities.*

▲ *The Commissioners engaged in their survey. The results were published in* Description de l'Egypte, *which reawakened interest in the area.*

▲ *Members of Napoleon's expedition measure the Sphinx, as depicted in a drawing by Vivant Denon from* Voyages dans le Basse et la Haute Egypte.

In addition, the Commission recorded several of the temples of Upper Egypt, with their unimaginable images still bright with colour. Apparently the sight of the Luxor and Karnak temples as they rounded a bend in the Nile so overwhelmed the troops with the expedition that they spontaneously 'formed ranks and presented arms to the accompaniment of the drums and the bands'. Metaphorically speaking, this must also have been the reaction of the intelligentsia of Europe as the volumes were published.

A popular version of the *Description,* the work of Vivant Denon, was published in 1802. This book, the *Voyages dans la Basse et la Haute Egypte,* became a great success. It ran to 40 editions and was also translated into English and German. The book brought the discoveries made in Egypt to a much wider readership and, together with the *Description de l'Egypte,* led to a wave of Egyptomania that swept across Europe. However, this renewed interest also sadly led to the unscrupulous looting of antiquities by private collectors and museums alike.

Vivant Denon

Egyptology owes a great deal to Baron Dominique Vivant Denon (1747–1825). He had served at court under Louis XV and also as ambassador of France at St Petersburg and Naples under Louis XVI and, despite his distinguished career, he managed to survive the French Revolution unscathed. The Empress Josephine, who found him a place on Napoleon's expedition to Egypt, later befriended him.

Denon proved himself to be a talented artist and undertook much of the Commission's illustrative work, albeit sometimes in very difficult conditions, surrounded by Mamelukes and Arabs taking potshots at him. He also complained at the little time he had at his disposal in the Valley of the Kings. Allowed only three hours to record six tombs, he exclaimed:

How was it possible to leave such precious curiosities, without taking a drawing of them? How to return without having at least a sketch to show? I earnestly demanded a quarter of an hour's grace: I was allowed twenty minutes; one person lighted me, while another held a taper to every object I pointed out to him, and I completed my task in the time prescribed with spirit and correctness.

On his return from Egypt, Denon was appointed Director General of Museums, and he went on later to found the Musée Napoléon, now the Louvre, in Paris. ◆

▼ *Vivant Denon, whose discourse and publications made a great contribution to the rise of Egyptology.*

European Rivalry: Champollion and Young

One of the most important antiquities to be studied as a result of Napoleon's expedition was the Rosetta Stone. This slab of black basalt was discovered in 1799, incorporated into an old wall, by a French officer inspecting the building of Fort Julien, near Rosetta in the Delta. After the French defeat, the British seized the stone and today it is in the British Museum, London.

The stone was inscribed in three different kinds of writing. One section was in Greek, which could be read, one was in Egyptian hieroglyphs and the other was in a cursive script. The race was soon on to decipher it. The main contestants were the French linguist Jean-François Champollion (1790–1832), his compatriot Sylvestre de Sacy (1758–1832), the English scientist Dr Thomas Young (1773–1829) and the Swedish diplomat Johan David Akerblad (1763–1819). Both Champollion and Young had been child prodigies and were conversant with Greek, Latin, Hebrew, Arabic and Aramaic, as well as several European languages.

Deciphering the hieroglyphs

All four scholars recognized the importance of the Rosetta Stone as the key to a modern understanding of the history and culture of ancient Egypt. Each had a copy of the three texts, but it was 20 years before any real progress was made. The Greek text proved to be a decree celebrating the anniversary of the coronation of Ptolemy V (205–180 BC). It was guessed that the other two sections of the inscription were versions of the same text. The first clue came in the name of Ptolemy. This could be read in Greek and was found in the hieroglyphic version inside a cartouche, the oval outline that, it was also guessed, enclosed the names of a king. Young compared this cartouche with two others inscribed on an obelisk that had been brought to England from Philae and is now in Kingston Lacy, Dorset. On this he was able to recognize the names of both Ptolemy and Cleopatra, since they have several letters in common. However, he failed to crack the code because he refused to believe that, apart from use in foreign names (the Ptolemies were Macedonian), the

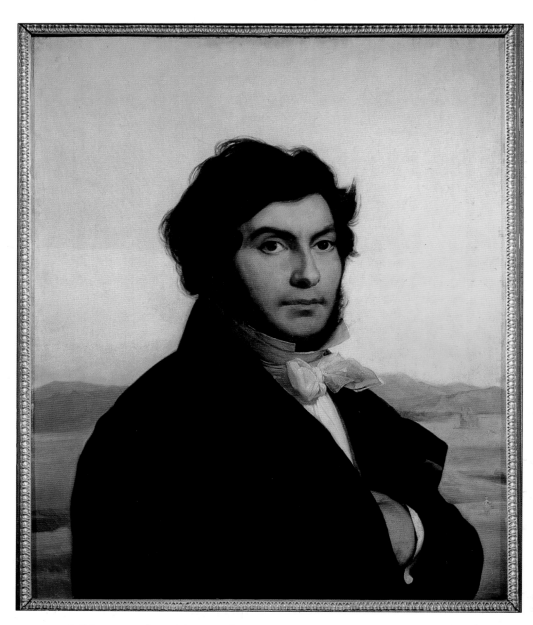

▲ *Jean-François Champollion did most to decipher Egyptian hieroglyphs by realizing that a sign could represent both an idea and a sound.*

hieroglyphs could have an alphabetic or phonetic value. He firmly believed that the hieroglyphs were symbols that conveyed the sense of a whole word. The breakthrough came when Champollion, aided by his knowledge of Coptic (the last written form of the ancient Egyptian

MONUMENTS
DE
L'EGYPTE
ET DE
LA NUBIE
PAR
CHAMPOLLION LE JEUNE

language, which employed mostly Greek characters), realized that hieroglyphs could convey both an idea and a sound value. In 1822, he was able to study some copies of texts from the temples of Tuthmosis III (c.1479–c.1425 BC) and Ramesses II (c.1279–1213 BC) in Nubia. Again, the royal names were identifiable because they were written in cartouches. These kings were also known from the classical authors, and Champollion was able to refer to Coptic to confirm his intuition about their identities and the way in which the language worked. He knew that *ra* means 'sun' in Coptic, and in the cartouche he saw a sun disc that

▶ *In 1828, Champollion travelled through Egypt and Nubia reading inscriptions. In this book he proved the accuracy of his decipherment.*

not only expressed the idea of 'sun' but the sound *ra* in Egyptian. He already knew the letter 's' from the Greek form of the name of Ptolemy (Ptolemaios). Guessing that the middle symbol was *mes,* he arrived at the name 'Ramesses'.

▼ *Written in Greek and ancient Egyptian, using three scripts (Greek, Egyptian hieroglyphs and demotic), the Rosetta Stone held the key to the decipherment of the ancient Egyptian texts.*

Champollion made his discoveries known in September 1822 in a lecture to the Paris Académie des Inscriptions et Belles Lettres, now famous as the *Lettre à M. Dacier.* He then went on to study as many texts as he could lay his hands on in Turin, Aix and Livorno, and at last fulfilled his ambition to visit Egypt. During his 15-month trip, he travelled from Alexandria to Abu Simbel and beyond, reading the ancient texts along the way. Each one confirmed the views he had expressed in his lecture. Writing to Dacier, he said:

Now that I have followed the course of the Nile from its mouth to the Second Cataract, I am in a position to tell you we need change nothing in our Alphabet of the Hieroglyphs, our alphabet is correct: it applies equally well to the Egyptian monuments built during the time of the Romans and the Ptolemies and – what is of much greater interest – to the inscriptions in all the temples, palaces and tombs dating from the time of the pharaohs.

Champollion was, however, scathing about the efforts of his rivals. Akerblad, he reckoned, could not read 'three words of an Egyptian inscription'. Although Young had made a valuable contribution to the decipherment of the Rosetta Stone, had correctly asserted that the second of the scripts was a cursive form of hieroglyphs and had published an article in the Encyclopaedia Britannica on the subject, Champollion dismissed his efforts as 'mere bragging'. For his part, Young refused to believe that Champollion had accurately cracked the code. ◆

The Race for the Antiquities

The discoveries that were made during Napoleon's expedition gave rise to a passion for all things Egyptian throughout Europe, and led to a lucrative trade in ancient artefacts, eagerly sought by both private collectors and public institutions. Major collectors of the antiquities could make large fortunes, and such was the competition between them that fights often broke out between the rival gangs of workers at the excavation sites.

Bernadino Drovetti

Drovetti had served as a colonel during Napoleon's expedition to Egypt. He became Consul General of Egypt in 1810, and for the next 19 years used his position to carve out a career as an antiques dealer. He often directed excavations himself and took an active

▼ *Belzoni's drawing of the Temple of Karnak. Only the tops of the pillars and pylons stood out from the mounds of accumulated sand and rubble.*

part in the looting of antiquities, ably assisted by his agent Jean-Jacques Rifaud, a sculptor from Marseilles. When he had amassed a significant collection he offered the finds to Louis XVIII, hoping that they would be bought for the Louvre in Paris. But the king thought the price too high, so Drovetti sold the collection to the King of Sardinia, who presented it to the Turin Museum in 1824. Some of the best pieces of royal sculpture, including the famous seated statue of Ramesses II (c.1279–c.1213 BC), are in this collection today and the Turin Museum was the first to own such an important group.

Drovetti then embarked on another collection, which he again offered to France. This time it was bought by Charles X, on the recommendation of Champollion, on behalf of the Louvre, where it became the nucleus of the Egyptian Antiquities section. Friedrich Wilhelm III of Prussia bought a third collection in 1836 for the Berlin Museum.

Henry Salt

Not to be outdone, the British Consul General, Henry Salt, also collected antiquities on the instructions of Sir Thomas Banks, one of the Trustees of the British Museum. However, he was bitterly disappointed when he was offered a mere £2,000 for what he had assembled. This did not even cover the cost of excavation and transport. Furthermore, the museum refused to buy the best item in the collection, the beautiful alabaster sarcophagus of Seti I (c.1294–c.1279 BC). This was later bought by Sir John Soane, who paid as much for it as Salt had received for the rest of the collection, and it is the centrepiece of Sir John Soane's Museum in Lincoln's Inn Fields, London.

A second collection made by Salt was offered to the British Museum, but was finally sold to king Charles X of France and presented to the Louvre. Among its many important pieces was the Karnak kinglist, which made the Louvre collection as important as that of Turin.

◄ *Bernardino Drovetti, standing centre left, whose collection formed the nucleus of the Turin Museum.*

'The Patagonian Samson'

Belzoni had enjoyed a varied career before entering Salt's service. At one time he had entertained ideas of becoming a monk, but he later appeared as 'The Patagonian Samson' in a music-hall act at Sadler's Wells Theatre in London. He was extremely tall and immensely strong, and the climax of his act was to appear on stage strapped into an iron harness carrying a dozen or so people who formed a 'human pyramid'.

Giovanni Belzoni

Salt's right-hand man in the difficult process of transporting the antiquities to Europe was the adventurer Giovanni Belzoni. He first visited Egypt in 1814 with the idea of interesting the Turkish viceroy, Mohammed Ali Pasha, in a water-raising device he had invented. Unfortunately for Belzoni his machine was rejected, and he was left penniless as he had sunk all his funds into the project. In despair, he left Cairo in 1816. But as luck would have it, he was approached by the scholar and explorer Jean-Louis Burckhardt, who introduced him to Salt. Burckhardt suggested that they should try to remove the colossal fallen bust of Ramesses II from the Ramesseum and transport it to England.

By means of four great levers the bust was raised sufficiently for a huge raft on rollers to be placed underneath it, and Ramesses began the first stage of his long, slow journey to London. It took ten days to cover less than 2km (1 mile). The local rulers put many difficulties in the way, but eventually the statue reached the River Nile.

While waiting for a ship big enough to carry the bust to Cairo, Belzoni used the time to visit the Valley of the Kings, where he explored the magnificent tomb of Seti I. Belzoni was also a talented artist and faithfully copied all the painted reliefs and texts he found in Seti's tomb. His drawings were later exhibited to great public acclaim in London and Paris. Even Champollion went to have a look at Belzoni's work and copied a number of the texts in support of his theories on decipherment.

During the wait for a ship, Belzoni also excavated at Karnak, where he discovered 18 statues of the lioness-headed goddess Sekhmet, a kneeling statue of Seti II (c.1200–c.1194 BC) and several sphinxes, all of which are today in the British Museum collections. Belzoni also took part in the excavation of Abu Simbel and made accurate records of the temple. ◆

▲ *Giovanni Belzoni, seen here in Turkish dress, was given money by the British Consul General to collect antiquities for the British Museum.*

▲ *Illustrations from a book by Belzoni of Karnak and a colossal statue, thought to be of Ramesses II, that he found there.*

The Founders of Egyptology

The nineteenth century saw the development of an ever-increasing body of serious travellers to Egypt. By this time, these travellers' main interest lay in making careful records of the antiquities, rather than in removing them from their original settings to the museums of Europe.

John Gardner Wilkinson

The work of Sir John Gardner Wilkinson (1797–1875) laid the foundations of Egyptology in Britain. Arriving in Egypt in 1821, he spent the next 12 years systematically studying the main archaeological sites of Egypt and Nubia, including Karnak, the tombs of the Valley of the Kings and Gebel Barkal, the sacred mountain near the Fourth Cataract. He made precise copies of the tombs at Beni Hasan, identified the 'Labyrinth' described by the classical authors as the mortuary temple of Amenemhat III (c.1855–c.1808 BC) at Hawara and was the first to draw up a detailed plan of Tell el-Amarna, the city of Akhenaten (c.1352–c.1336 BC). Some of his most valuable work was in the field of epigraphy, which is the study of ancient inscriptions. He made exact copies of the texts he came across during his excavations, and identified the names of many of the ancient Egyptian kings for the first time. The detailed precision of his work far out-classed that of his contemporaries, and it remains a veritable mine of information for modern Egyptologists.

Wilkinson was interested in more than the monuments, however, and on his return to England wrote a massive work entitled *The Manners and Customs of the Ancient Egyptians.* Using his copies of scenes from the tombs, papyri and other inscriptional material, he produced a vivid portrayal of the daily life of the ancient Egyptians. Later, he made a detailed study of the famous kinglist known as the Turin Canon, and helped to establish the correct order of the rulers of ancient Egypt.

▼ *A watercolour painting by Lepsius depicts the city of Thebes, showing the ruins of the temples of Luxor and Karnak.*

▶ *John Gardner Wilkinson was the first British scholar to make a science of Egyptology. He was particularly famous for his copies of tombs and their inscriptions.*

Tanis, he discovered the Canopus Decree: this document, written in Greek and Demotic, proved useful to scholars engaged in decipherment because it could be compared with the Rosetta Stone. Until his death in 1884, Lepsius produced many more publications, and was also the editor of the leading German Egyptological journal, the *Zeitschrift für ägyptische Sprache und Altertumskunde*. Lepsius did more than anyone else to put Germany, particularly the Berlin Museum, on the map in the field of Egyptology. ◆

▼ *The antiquities and 15,000 casts Lepsius brought home from Egypt formed the nucleus of the Berlin Museum's Egyptian collection.*

Carl Richard Lepsius

In 1842, Carl Lepsius (1810–84) was commissioned by Friedrich Wilhelm IV of Prussia to lead an expedition to Egypt. Before this he had spent years studying Champollion's grammar in order to learn hieroglyphs, and had visited the major European collections of Egyptian antiquities. As with the earlier expeditions, Lepsius' main task was to record the monuments and to take home antiquities. His team included the artist Joseph Bonomi and the English architect James Wild. On his return he published his findings in a monumental work, *Denkmäler aus Aegypten und Aethiopien* (1849–58), a book comparable in scale to Napoleon's *Description de l'Egypte*.

Lepsius' work is particularly important because it describes many sites where there was considerably more to see at the time of his visit than there is today. Many of them have suffered at the hands of looters as well as from the ravages of time. In fact, some of the most important finds of recent times came about through his work. Professor Geoffrey Martin's rediscovery of the tombs of Maya, Tutankhamun's treasurer, and the king's general, Horemheb, were made possible by surveys and descriptions made by Lepsius of the tombs at Saqqara dating from the New Kingdom (c.1550–c.1069 BC). They lay buried beneath the sand as the joint expedition of the Egypt Exploration Society and the National Museum of Antiquities in Leiden set to work in 1975.

In 1865, Lepsius was rewarded with the post of Keeper of the Egyptian Antiquities Department in the Berlin Museum, and some months later he led another expedition to Egypt, this time to the little-explored area of the Delta. At

Mariette and French Egyptology

Auguste Mariette (1821–81) first became interested in Egyptology in 1842 while he was sorting through some papers left to his family by his cousin Nestor L'Hôte. L'Hôte had accompanied Napoleon's expedition to Egypt and had produced several drawings for Champollion, some as yet unpublished. Mariette spent the next seven years learning hieroglyphs and studying Coptic before finding employment in the Louvre, where he made an inventory of all the museum's ancient Egyptian texts.

The Serapaeum

In 1850, Mariette was sent to Egypt to collect papyri, but because he was given a rather lukewarm reception in the monasteries of the Wadi Natrun he decided to try his luck elsewhere. He eventually arrived at Saqqara, the cemetery site for the ancient capital Memphis. On seeing a sphinx half-buried in the sand he was immediately reminded of the words of Strabo:

There is also a Serapaeum at Memphis, in a place so sandy that dunes of sand are heaped up by the winds: and by these, some of the sphinxes which I saw were buried even to the head and others were half visible; from which one might guess the danger if a sandstorm should fall upon a man travelling on foot towards the temple.

Mariette felt irresistibly led by these words towards the Serapaeum, which was the burial place of the mummified remains of the Apis bulls. Each of these sacred animals was regarded during its lifetime as the representation on earth of the deity Apis (a manifestation of Ptah, the creator god of Memphis) and was kept in a special stall near his temple. After death the bulls were associated with the Underworld gods Sokar and Osiris, and were laid to rest at Saqqara.

The avenue leading to the temple took two years to clear and it was only in the face of much official opposition that

◀ Auguste Mariette, the founder of the Egyptian Antiquities Service and the Bulaq (now Cairo) Museum. He discovered the Serapaeum, the burial place of the Apis bulls, and the valley temple of the Old Kingdom king Khafre, at Giza.

Mariette was allowed to complete his work in the Serapaeum itself. However, he was eventually able to restore some kind of order to the chaos found in the subterranean passages and burial chambers, where the sarcophagus lids had been prised off and many had been smashed. The Serapaeum subsequently became a major tourist attraction and its discovery brought Mariette much acclaim. He often conducted important visitors to the Serapaeum in person and on such occasions the galleries were lit by hundreds of children carrying candles, giving an effect described as dreamlike and magical. Inside the last burial chamber, the guests found a table set with silver goblets and a bottle of champagne, with folding chairs ready to receive them.

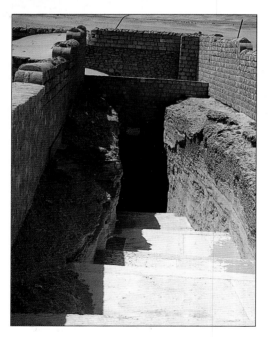

▲ Mariette's discovery in the Serapaeum of an undisturbed Apis burial, with the bull's mummy, jewellery and gold, brought him worldwide fame.

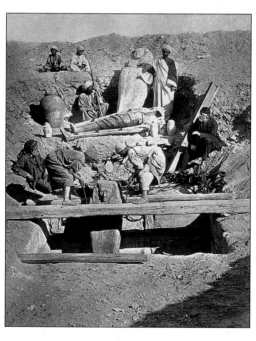

▲ Mariette's excavation methods are criticized today. He often requisitioned the male population of villages to further the work and used dynamite.

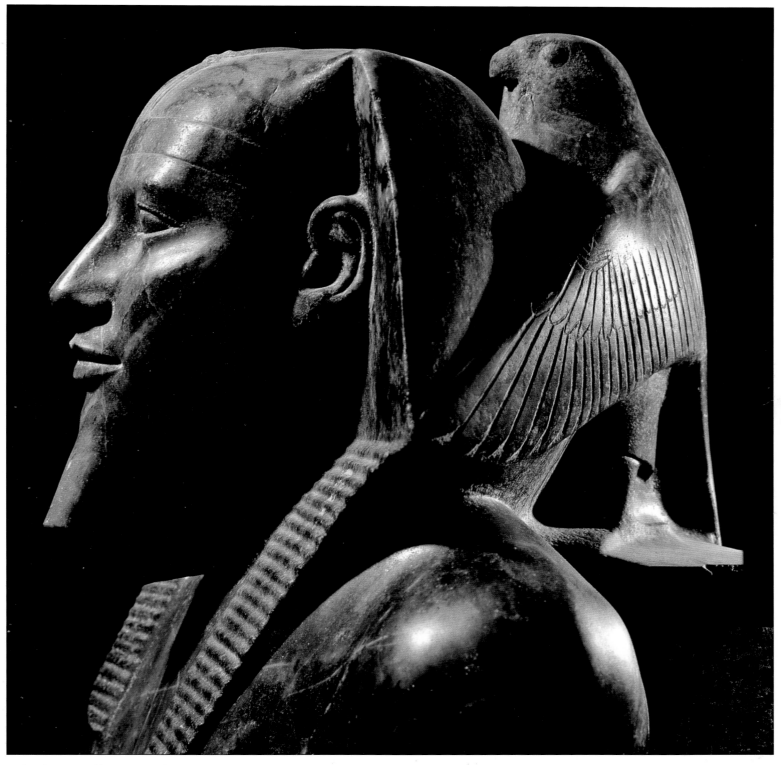

Khafre's valley temple

Mariette's second most important discovery was the valley temple of the pyramid of the Fourth Dynasty king Khafre (c.2558–c.2532 BC) at Giza. At the time of its discovery, it had been virtually reduced to a heap of enormous stones. He began work on it in 1853, when he partly excavated the interior, and completed it in 1858. In the course of the excavation he blew apart some of the collapsed monoliths in order to remove them from the temple. He is often criticized for the fact that here, as elsewhere, he failed to publish his finds adequately. But in this case he did discover one of the masterpieces of the Old Kingdom (c.2686–c.2181 BC), the great diorite statue of Khafre himself (now in the Cairo Museum).

▲ *Found by Mariette in the valley temple, this diorite statue of King Khafre protected by the hawk god Horus is a masterpiece of Egyptian art.*

In 1858, Mariette was appointed Director of the Egyptian Antiquities Service, and the viceroy gave him the authority and means to excavate wherever he wished. He set up the Bulaq Museum near Cairo to exhibit his finds. ◆

Amelia Edwards

It was entirely by chance that Amelia Edwards (1831–92) first became interested in Egypt. She and a friend had gone to France on a sketching holiday and had been plagued by weeks of rain. After discussing whether to return to England or 'push on further still in search of sunshine', they decided to go to Egypt. She later wrote:

For in simple truth we had drifted hither by accident with no excuse of health or business or any serious object whatsoever and had just taken refuge in Egypt as one might turn aside into the Burlington Arcade... to get out of the rain.

In spite of this rather prosaic start to her relationship with Egypt, once she was there it was clearly a case of love at first sight. On looking out of her window on the first morning of her stay she was immediately captivated by the scene:

It was dark last night, and I had no idea that my room overlooked an enchanted garden, far-reaching and solitary, peopled with stately giants beneath whose tufted crowns hung

rich clusters of maroon and amber dates... Yonder, between the pillared stems, rose the minaret of a very distant mosque; and here where the garden was bounded by a wall and a windowless house, I saw a veiled lady walking on the terraced roof in the midst of a cloud of pigeons. Nothing could be more simple than the scene and its accessories; nothing at the same time more Eastern, strange, and unreal.

Before going to Egypt, Amelia Edwards had already achieved some success as a writer and journalist. She was to become one of the most prominent writers of her age, and her work included several travel books, the most famous of which is the record of her six-month journey up the River Nile, *A Thousand Miles up the Nile*.

A Thousand Miles up the Nile

It is typical of Edwards' enterprise and courage that she and her friend decided to make the most of their trip to Egypt by chartering a *dahabeeyah* (a flat-bottomed, wooden boat) and engaging a crew with a view to sailing up the Nile

▲ *Amelia Edwards wrote the best-selling book* A Thousand Miles Up the Nile *(1877) and founded what is now the Egypt Exploration Society.*

to Aswan and then beyond the borders of Egypt into Nubia. This was in 1873, the year David Livingstone died and before General Gordon had made his first journey to Khartoum, a remarkable feat for two women at that time.

By far the greater part of *A Thousand Miles up the Nile* is devoted to the monuments she visited. The modern tourist sees them in their reconstructed state, but when Edwards went to Egypt over a century ago, many of the tombs and temples were filled with the rubble and driven sand of past centuries. Describing the ruins of Luxor Temple she wrote:

These half-buried pylons, this solitary obelisk, those giant heads rising in ghastly resurrection before the gates of the temple were magnificent still. But it was as the magnificence of the

◀ *A 19th-century painting of the Cairo Bazaar that so fascinated Amelia Edwards on her arrival.*

Preparing for the voyage

The hiring of Edwards' *dahabeeyah* was much more difficult than house-hunting. Added to the problems of weighing up the merits of the available boats was the fact that they frequently changed their position on the river. The prices varied from day to day and the 'certificates of recommendation' by former travellers had 'a mysterious way of turning up again and again on board different boats and in the hands of different claimants'.

Eventually Edwards and her friend found a craft to their liking. After scurrying to the nearest stores to make a few last-minute purchases, they went on board and set about transforming the sparsely furnished saloon of the *dahabeeyah* into a cosy Victorian parlour. As Edwards remarked, 'It is wonderful what a few books and roses, an open piano and a sketch or two will do'.

prologue to a poem of which only garbled fragments remain. Beyond that entrance lay a smoky, filthy, intricate labyrinth of lanes and passages. Mud hovels, mud pigeon houses, mud yards, and a mud mosque, clustered like wasps' nests in and about the ruins. Architraves sculptured with royal titles supported the roofs of squalid cabins. Stately capitals peeped out from the midst of sheds in which buffaloes, camels, donkeys, dogs and human beings were huddled together in unsavoury fellowship.

Edwards began work on the book on her return to England in 1874. She read extensively and consulted respected Egyptologists on matters of historical and archaeological detail. She also took up the study of hieroglyphs. By 1878, she was writing reviews and articles on Egyptology for weekly journals such as The Academy, and quickly became an authority in her own right.

The Egypt Exploration Fund

Amelia Edwards' greatest work was the founding of the Egypt Exploration Fund (now Society). She was very concerned about the state of the ancient monuments; many were suffering from neglect; others were being vandalized. The Egyptian government had neither the interest nor the resources necessary to protect them. In 1879, Edwards wrote to Auguste Mariette, the founder of the Cairo (Bulaq) Museum, to ask if it might be possible to finance excavation in the Delta by public subscription in England. She also enlisted the support of several English Egyptologists and Biblical scholars.

Edwards' most enthusiastic supporter was Sir Erasmus Wilson, an eminent surgeon who was already engaged in writing a popular history of Egypt. He was also very wealthy and had just spent £10,000 transporting the obelisk now known as Cleopatra's Needle to England. When *A Thousand Miles up the Nile* was published, Wilson was so impressed with it that he wrote to Edwards, and thus began a long friendship. She advised him on his book and he was always willing to give financial support to any scientific survey or excavation by the British in Egypt. Others were less easy to persuade. The Oriental Department of the British Museum was totally opposed to Edwards' efforts, although help came

▲ *Nile cruises became very popular after the publication of Amelia Edwards' book.*

from elsewhere in the Museum, notably from the Department of Coins and Medals. The Egypt Exploration Fund was eventually set up in March 1882, with R. S. Poole and Amelia Edwards as Honorary Secretaries and Sir Erasmus Wilson as Treasurer.

The Fund found many supporters in the United States, where Edwards embarked on an extensive and exhausting lecture tour in 1889. During the five months she was there, she lectured 115 times and travelled to 16 different states. Her labours were well rewarded and the subscriptions flowed in.

First chair in Egyptology

The strenuous tour of North America had left Edwards' health seriously impaired, but her devotion to the Fund impelled her to go to Millwall Docks in London in October 1891 to supervise the arrival of antiquities from Egypt and their dispersal to various museums. A lung infection resulted, from which she never recovered. She died the following spring, bequeathing a sum of money to found the first chair in Egyptology at University Collge, London, with the proviso that Flinders Petrie should be the first professor. ◆

The Father of Modern Egyptology

Sir William Matthew Flinders Petrie (1853–1942) was the pioneer of modern archaeological methods in Egypt. In great contrast to his contemporaries, his main anxiety was to halt the destruction of the ancient remains.

Petrie had received little formal education but his father had taught him the principles of surveying and geometry. After practising on Stonehenge, father and son planned to visit Egypt to survey the Great Pyramid. In the end, his father did not go, and Petrie undertook the task alone. Nobody had ever done anything like it before. He spent several weeks setting up the survey points and making accurate plans, which he published in 1883. He also spent much time weighing up the possible methods by which the pyramids might have been constructed.

He was horrified by what he saw going on in the valley temple of Khafre:

Mariette most rascally blasted to pieces all the fallen parts of the granite temple by a large gang of soldiers, to clear it out instead of lifting the stones and replacing them by means of tackle… Nothing seems to be done with any uniform and regular plan, work is begun and left unfinished; no regard is paid to future requirements of exploration, and no civilized or labour-saving devices are used. It is sickening to see the rate at which everything is being destroyed, and the little regard paid to preservation.

In his time, Petrie excavated at most of the important archaeological sites. He worked principally at the Predynastic cemeteries at Naqada, the Delta sites of Tanis and Naucratis, the city of Akhenaten at Tell el-Amarna, the Faiyum pyramids of Senusret II (c.1880–c.1874 BC) and Amenemhat III (c.1855–c.1808 BC), and the remains of the cemetery and ancient city of Abydos.

▲ *Flinders Petrie, the pioneer of modern archaeological methods in Egypt and the first Professor of Egyptology at University College, London.*

Excavations at Abydos

Although frustrated in his ambition for many years, in 1899 Petrie was eventually granted the concession to dig at Abydos. There he found that the site had been dug over many times, both by dealers and by local farmers looking for mudbrick to grind up for use as fertilizer on their land. Mariette had removed statues from the site for the Bulaq Museum. Worst of all, the Frenchman Emile Clément Amélineau had worked over the royal tombs of the Early Dynastic Period (c.3100–c.2686 BC) and had done untold damage in the process. It had been rumoured that he was interested only in large, intact, saleable objects and that he broke those he was not able to carry away: Petrie found that this appeared to be true. Moreover, because Amélineau had treated his workmen badly and offered them no reward for objects they found, there seemed to have been much pilfering from the site.

When Petrie began to rework the site, he found much that Amélineau had missed, including some of the grave stelae that marked the royal tombs and small tablets indicating the graves of officials. Most important of all were the little ivory and ebony labels originally attached to grave goods, which gave the

▼ *The members of Petrie's teams led a spartan life. At the age of 83, Petrie and his wife Hilda (in the helmet) used this old green bus in Palestine.*

▲ *Ivory comb of King Djet from the Early Dynastic cemetery at Abydos.*

names of some of the kings, each one recording an important event in a particular year of the king's reign. From these, Petrie was able to collect the names of all the kings of the First Dynasty (c.3100–c.2890 BC) and to suggest the order in which they had reigned.

During his excavation of the tomb of King Djer (c.3000 BC), Petrie found part of an arm wrapped in bandages, later found to be wearing a set of four exquisite bracelets made of gold, lapis lazuli, amethyst and turquoise. After carefully examining the jewellery, he entrusted the precious burden to James Quibell, the Chief Inspector of Antiquities for Lower Egypt, to deliver to the Cairo Museum. However, the museum's assistant conservator was interested only in the jewellery, and threw away the arm and the linen, thus destroying the earliest evidence for mummification. As Petrie remarked, 'a museum is a dangerous place'.

This discovery also demonstrates the superior way in which Petrie treated his workers. He always believed in paying his men properly for anything that they

found so that he could be sure they would bring their finds to him rather than take them to the dealers. In this instance, the workmen could see the jewellery inside the wrappings, but left the arm undisturbed while they went to find one of Petrie's assistants. In the evening, the arm was unwrapped in the presence of the workmen and the gold of the bracelets weighed against sovereigns. The men were paid handsomely 'to ensure their goodwill and honesty for the future'.

Petrie's interest in objects of everyday life also marks him as remarkably astute. In his day, these would usually have been passed over in favour of the more spectacular. From the small finds made at Kahun, the settlement of the workers on Senusret II's pyramid at el-Lahun, it is possible to build up a complete picture of life within the community.

Honeymoon on a coal barge

Petrie was aided in his work by his wife, Hilda Urlin, one of his former students. Their wedding breakfast, a glass of milk and a bun at a café opposite Victoria Station in London, before catching the boat-train to Calais on the first stage of their journey to Egypt, anticipated the austerity of their married life. After nearly two weeks in Cairo they set off for Dendera. The train went no farther than Nag' Hamadi, so they hired a boat for the rest of the journey. Unfortunately, the wind dropped and they were forced to spend the night in cramped conditions under the half deck. They breakfasted on the remains of the previous night's supper of bread, 'little fritters', beans and jam. A colleague, Norman de Garis Davies, was with them, and all three had to share a single knife and tin mug provided by the boatmen. When they were still 16km (10 miles) from their destination at two in the afternoon, they decided to walk the rest of the way. Hilda claimed to have enjoyed this 'most delightful adventure' of her 'honeymoon on a coal barge'. ◆

▲ *This carved ivory label was once attached to a pair of sandals from the royal cemetery at Abydos. King Den is shown smiting his enemies.*

Sequence dating

Petrie devised an ingenious method, called sequence dating, of putting into chronological order the finds from his excavations at Naqada, Hu and Abadlya. He cut 900 strips of cardboard, each 17cm (7in) long, to represent 900 of the 4,000 tombs he had excavated. On each he recorded the number of pots of various types he had found in the grave, as well as other objects such as palettes and beads. By comparing the contents of each grave, he was able to work out a probable chronological order. Assuming that designs would become more complex over time, Petrie assigned the earliest sequence dates to the simplest artefacts, using a numerical sequence from 30–80 (the numbers 1–29 were kept free in case earlier objects were found). He was able to divide the pottery and associated grave goods into two main phases, now usually called Naqada I (c.4000–c.3500 BC; red pottery with white decoration) and Naqada II (c.3500–c.3100 BC; buff-coloured pottery decorated with red motifs such as ships, ostriches and dancing women). Although adjustments have been made in the light of more recent discoveries, the system is still used by archaeologists today.

The Development of the Pyramid Complex

The Predynastic Period in Egypt lasted from around the mid-sixth millennium BC to c.3100 BC. During this long, formative period, the many individual cultures of different parts of Egypt were gradually replaced by those now called Naqada II (c.3500–c.3100 BC) and III (c.3100–c.3000 BC). Naqada was a site in the south of Egypt excavated by Sir Flinders Petrie in 1895, and it gave its name to a particular type of burial that had distinctive grave goods. At the same time, the various settlement centres gradually developed into a politically unified state ruled by a king.

Some of the most impressive archaeological remains of the Early Dynastic Period (c.3100–c.2686 BC) are the mudbrick mastabas, or burial places, of the kings and their officials at Saqqara, Abydos and Naqada. Mastaba, from an Arabic word meaning 'bench', is the name given to a type of tomb that looks rather like the mudbrick benches seen outside Egyptian houses. The burial chamber was below ground, surrounded by storerooms filled with goods for the use of the deceased in the Afterlife. Above ground, a mudbrick super-structure was built with an offering chapel attached. In later examples, the offering chapel was incorporated into the superstructure. It was from these mastaba tombs that the later royal pyramid complexes developed, while the mastaba form continued to be used by high-ranking officials whose burial places were usually clustered around those of the kings they had served.

◀ *Amenemhat III's pyramid at Hawara was the last large pyramid to be built in Egypt.*

Early Dynastic Period Mastabas

The earliest type of mastaba had a pit cut into the desert plateau. This was divided by mudbrick walls into the burial chamber and storerooms. There was no way into the burial chamber from outside, so the tomb was finished only after the burial had taken place. Later in the Early Dynastic Period, access to the burial place was provided by a staircase leading into the tomb, so it could be constructed before the body was buried. Precautions against robbers were apparently necessary, because in several tombs portcullises blocked the stairway.

During the Old Kingdom (c.2686–c.2181 BC) the storerooms were incorporated into the superstructure, from which a shaft led down to the burial chamber below ground. Stones often blocked the shaft. The main offering niche also became part of the internal plan, and eventually developed into a funerary chapel, decorated with scenes depicting the life of the tomb owner.

Abydos

As recently as about a century ago, the history of the earliest dynasties was still unknown. Flinders Petrie described the

▲ *These two small dolomite vases with gold lids fastened with gold wire came from the tomb of the 2nd Dynasty king Khasekhemwy at Abydos.*

period before King Sneferu (c.2613–c.2589 BC), first king of the Fourth Dynasty, as 'a blank', but he did more than any other Egyptologist to fill the gap, with his discoveries in the First and Second Dynasty mastaba tombs of Abydos. Emile Amélineau had excavated these between 1894–8, but much had been missed. Petrie re-dug the site much more meticulously and was able to chart the development of the architecture of the tombs, which he was convinced were

the burial places of the earliest kings. He also found objects inscribed with the names of previously unknown kings and was able to suggest a tentative chronology. This has recently been confirmed by the find at Abydos, by a team from the German Archaeological Institute led by Gunther Dreyer, of a clay seal, giving the names of the first five kings of the dynasty in order. The members of the team have continued the work on architectural

▼ *Remains of 1st and 2nd Dynasty tombs discovered by Walter B. Emery at Saqqara; thought to be royal tombs when first excavated, they are now known to have belonged to officials.*

development, and have found evidence for several stages of building in some tombs. They have also studied the links between the Early Dynastic Period tombs and those of the Predynastic Period nearby. They are now postulating a Dynasty Zero preceding the First Dynasty, thus pushing back the boundaries of the known history of Egypt.

Graves of a typical Predynastic type have been found in Cemetery U at Abydos. Here, graves of the Naqada I and II and later periods have been found. Some Predynastic tombs of the latest stage have several chambers, and it is thought that these belonged to the Dynasty Zero kings. One originally had nine rooms, but was later extended to 12. The storerooms were filled with large numbers of pottery vases, some of local origin and others imported from Canaan. In the burial chamber were traces of a wooden shrine and an ivory sceptre very similar to those that later formed part of the royal insignia.

The first tombs of the Early Dynastic Period (c.3100–c.2686 BC) were found in Cemetery B. The most elaborate belonged to King Aha, probably the second king of the First Dynasty. This tomb too, seems to have been extended at various times. Surrounding the tomb were a large number of subsidiary graves for retainers. From a study of the skeletal remains it seems that the bodies were all of young men aged about 25, and that they were killed in order to accompany their royal master to the Afterlife.

The remaining First Dynasty tombs lie a little to the west. They, too, were brick-lined pits but some also had a further lining of wood panelling. They were also surrounded by the graves of servants. The superstructures have long since disappeared, but the grave markers remain, carved with the names of their royal owners.

Lying some distance away from the tombs themselves are the associated funerary enclosures, which were probably used for the funerary cults of the dead kings. Of those belonging to the First Dynasty kings little remains, but some that belonged to the kings of the Second Dynasty are still impressive. The best preserved belonged to King Khasekhemwy (c.2686 BC), and its double walls still stand to a considerable height. The outer surface of the inner wall is built in the 'palace façade' style, with a series of elaborate niches and false doors. Just inside the entrance to the enclosure were some small buildings. The funerary complexes, together with the tombs themselves, may well be the prototype of the Step Pyramid. A further clue may lie in the fact that the entrance to each of the Abydos enclosures is on the south-eastern corner, just like the entrance to the Step Pyramid complex.

Saqqara

Between 1936–56, Walter B. Emery found further mastaba tombs at Saqqara, the chief necropolis of Memphis. These had many rooms containing high-quality grave goods arranged around a central burial chamber. The fact that the tombs

▲ *The grave marker of King Djet from his tomb at Abydos. The* serekh *bearing his name is surmounted by Horus, thus associating the king with the god.*

were much bigger than those at Abydos (excluding the funerary enclosures) led Emery to think that he had found the true royal tombs at Saqqara, and that the tombs at Abydos were cenotaphs only. This theory has now been discounted, and the Saqqara tombs seem to have belonged to high officials. First, the number of tombs at Saqqara was much larger than the number of known kings, and second, seal impressions bearing the names of the same rulers turned up in several tombs. These seals were also inscribed with the names of senior officials. In the case of Mereruka, an official of the First Dynasty king Qa'a (c.2890 BC), a stela bearing his name was found near the main offering niche, making ownership of the tomb clear. This stela was the forerunner of the decoration of the false door of later funerary chapels and of the tomb autobiography, which was intended to justify the life of the deceased and provide his passport to immortality. ◆

The tomb of Djer

According to ancient Egyptian tradition, Abydos was the burial place of Osiris and, in the late Middle Kingdom (c.2055–c.1650 BC), the tomb of the First Dynasty king Djer (c.3000 BC) was remodelled as the god's tomb. Emile Amélineau found a stone statue representing Osiris lying on his side (a reference to the myth in which the god was killed by his jealous brother Seth). However, much of the original burial remained and Petrie, during his re-excavation of the site, found the now famous set of four bracelets still attached to part of a mummified arm.

The First Architecture in Stone

Until the beginning of the Third Dynasty (c.2686 BC), the main building materials were wood, reeds and mudbrick. The first building in the world to be constructed completely in stone was the Step Pyramid of King Djoser (c.2667–c.2648 BC) at Saqqara. Before this time, only a few details, such as doorways or the paving of a tomb chamber, had been made of stone. According to Manetho (an Egyptian priest who wrote a history of Egypt in the third century BC to impress Ptolemy II with the great splendour and antiquity of the civilization he had inherited), the inventor of the art of building in stone was Imhotep. That he was at any rate in charge of building operations at the Step Pyramid is clear from the discovery there of the pedestal of a statue of King Djoser bearing the words: 'The Chancellor of the King of Lower Egypt, the first after the King of Upper Egypt, Administrator of the Great Palace, Hereditary Lord, the High Priest of Heliopolis, Imhotep, the builder, the sculptor'.

Djoser's Step Pyramid

The Step Pyramid itself developed from the mudbrick royal mastabas of the Early Dynastic Period (c.3100–c.2686 BC) at Abydos. There, a mound of sand covered the burial chamber, perhaps representing

▲ *The Step Pyramid of King Djoser (c.2667– c.2648 BC), the world's first stone-built building. Previously, wood, reeds and mudbrick were used.*

the first land that appeared from the primordial ocean and on which creation took place, thus linking the themes of creation and re-creation. The mudbrick mastaba developed into a stone-built tower, and the mound became a ladder, which the king would climb to join the 'imperishable stars', a claim made in the Pyramid Texts, the funerary texts that accompanied royal burials during the Late Old Kingdom and First Intermediate Period (c.2350–c.2055 BC).

In the Step Pyramid complex, architecture that had previously been carried out in mudbrick, wood and reeds has been translated into stone. The wall surrounding the whole complex is built of small blocks of dressed limestone in

imitation of the mudbrick 'palace façade' style of Early Dynastic tombs and enclosure walls.

The entrance to the complex is at its south-eastern corner. Roofing in ancient Egypt was usually in the form of palm logs, and the entrance passage was roofed with such 'logs' copied in stone. There are no real doors at the actual entrance, but the vestibule has carvings in stone of huge wooden doors, forever open. Even the hinges have been reproduced, and the right-hand door has a slit to show which panel should be 'closed' first.

Inside the entrance stands a colonnade of 20 pairs of half-engaged columns. These imitate huge bound bundles of reeds. Although no buildings in this medium have survived in Egypt, until very recently the Marsh Arabs of southern Iraq used reeds to build their homes and strengthened the corners of buildings with reed bundles. Similar buildings are also known from Sumerian seals of the third millennium BC. It is

◀ *Papyrus plants made of stone, with triangular stems and open umbels, form half-engaged columns and capitals in the Northern Court.*

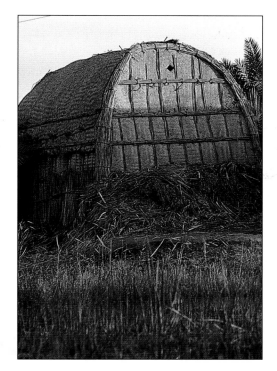

▲ *Bundles of reeds are used by the Marsh Arabs of southern Iraq to strengthen buildings. Stone versions were used in the Step Pyramid buildings.*

sometimes said that the Step Pyramid columns are half-engaged (joined to the wall) because the architect, uncertain of the new technique, was not sure that they would be strong enough to support the roof if they were free-standing. It is much more likely that they were direct copies of the way reed columns were used in house construction.

Dummy shrines

Plant forms are much in evidence elsewhere in the complex. The dummy buildings of the *heb sed* court and North and South Houses are translations into stone of different types of shrines to local gods, which until this time had been made of wood and reeds. The most common type represents a rectangular wooden-framed tent with an arched roof. The shrine stands on a pedestal. The curved roofs of the larger ones are supported with poles carved in imitation of the trunks of conifers. The poles suggest that the actual shrines were open at the front to reveal the image of the

▶ *Stone shrines to house statues of the gods surround the* heb sed *court where the king would be able to celebrate his jubilee in the Afterlife.*

god. They would have been temporary rather than permanent structures in real life, providing a shelter for the god's image at festivals.

The second type of shrine, seen in the North and South Houses of the complex, was larger and stood directly on the ground. These shrines, too, were open-fronted but the image of the god was shielded by a reed screen between the poles over the lower part of the building. The fact that reeds were actually used in this way in the construction of real reed shrines is suggested by the carving of their knotted ends. This stylized knotting became a standard architectural motif known as the *kheker* frieze.

In the third version of the temporary shrine, of which Temple T is an example, all four walls are plain and are strengthened at the corners by bound reed bundles. Another roll lies across the top of the wall, but here the loose ends of the reeds form a plain frieze. Inside, however, is another building, imitating one made of mudbrick.

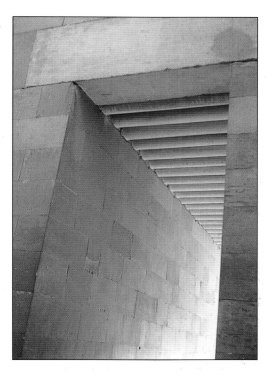

▲ *Palm-log ceilings are still features of Egyptian village houses. Stone imitations were used in the entrance lobby of the Step Pyramid complex.*

All these designs, including the double shrine, became features of later ancient Egyptian temple architecture, as did the papyrus column and open papyrus capital first seen in engaged form decorating the walls of the Northern Court. ◆

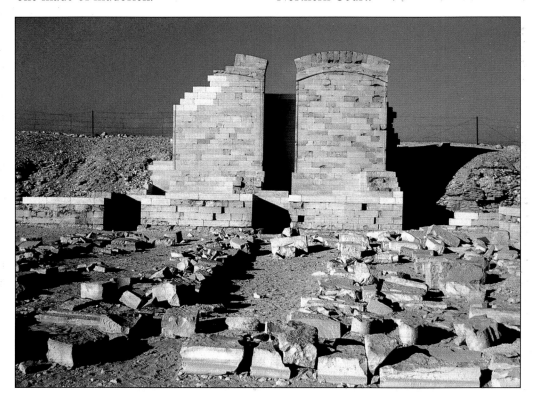

From Step Pyramid to True Pyramid

Two of Djoser's successors, Sekhemkhet (c.2648–c.2640 BC) and Khaba (c.2640–c.2637 BC), attempted to build step pyramid complexes but failed to complete them. There are also some provincial step pyramids, including one at Seila on the fringe of the Faiyum Oasis. It has been suggested that this may have belonged to the first king of the Fourth Dynasty, Sneferu (c.2613–c.2589 BC), which would bring the number of pyramids associated with him to four. Five of the step pyramids are tentatively associated with Huni (c.2637–c.2613 BC), Sneferu's predecessor. However, later kings did not copy this type of royal burial, although some features were incorporated into pyramid complexes belonging to later periods.

The Meidum Pyramid

Sneferu's three main pyramids were built at Meidum and Dahshur. Today, the Meidum Pyramid appears across the cultivation as a ghostly three-staged tower surrounded by a great heap of debris. It is often suggested either that the pyramid collapsed in antiquity, leaving the first stages of the building revealed, or that later builders used the pyramid as a quarry. Even the ownership of the pyramid is sometimes disputed. In the past, some scholars preferred to believe it was the work of Huni (largely because, at the time, no other pyramid had been attributed to him). However, all the texts found at the site, albeit from later periods, mention Sneferu rather than his predecessor, and as the ancient name of Meidum is Djed Sneferu ('Sneferu endures'), it seems likely that the pyramid belonged to him. The fact that the two stelae found in the mortuary chapel were uninscribed is rather a puzzle. Not only would a name have definitely established ownership but it was also considered extremely important in ancient Egyptian funerary

belief to perpetuate the name of the deceased, otherwise he might cease to exist in the Afterlife.

Sneferu began work on the Meidum Pyramid early in his reign. It was originally conceived as a seven-stepped tower, but a further step was added later. This seems to have been completed by Sneferu's 14th year but then, probably during the latter part of his reign, Sneferu had the steps filled in to form a true pyramid.

The Meidum Pyramid complex set the pattern for the rest of the Old Kingdom (c.2686–c.2181 BC). It consisted of the main pyramid and at least one subsidiary pyramid within an enclosure, together with a mortuary temple, to ensure the king's immortality. This was connected by a causeway to the valley, or lower,

▲ *It is possible that the Meidum Pyramid was never finished, explaining its present appearance. This may be why the stelae are uninscribed.*

temple, situated at the edge of the flood plain. The valley temple was linked to the River Nile by a canal, so that the funeral procession of the king could land here and the body be taken up the covered causeway for burial within the pyramid in relative privacy. The Meidum Pyramid is also remarkable for the first use of corbelling to roof the burial chamber.

The pyramids of Dahshur

For some unknown reason, in mid-reign Sneferu temporarily abandoned Meidum and began to build two further pyramids, the Bent and the Red Pyramids, further north, at the new necropolis of Dahshur.

▲ *The Bent Pyramid is so-called because of the change of angle about halfway up. Much of the high-quality Tura limestone casing remains.*

The Bent Pyramid seems to have been something of an experiment as the angles had not yet been satisfactorily worked out. There is evidence to suggest that the Bent Pyramid began as a small pyramid with a slope of 60 degrees, but that subsidence threatened to cause it to collapse. Thereupon further layers were added round the inner core so that the angle was more gentle. The problems continued, however, and it was eventually decided to proceed at an even less severe angle. Consequently the profile of the pyramid has a distinct bend towards the top.

The Bent Pyramid is noteworthy for the large amount of outer casing of fine Tura limestone that remains in situ. Further, both the burial chamber and the antechamber of the Bent Pyramid are roofed in magnificent corbelling. The mortuary chapel, on the other hand, is a very simple affair. Inside were an offering table and two stelae, both inscribed with the name of Sneferu. However, it was in the valley temple that Sneferu's funerary cult was carried out by later kings.

The Red Pyramid is perfectly constructed. There is no sign of experimentation whatsoever, and it is generally recognized as the first true pyramid. It was built of local limestone containing iron oxide, which gives it the reddish colour from which it gets its name. The outer casing of white Tura limestone has almost entirely

disappeared, but the pyramid is otherwise intact. Noteworthy features are the low angle of inclination (43 degrees) and the horizontal line of the core blocks. In earlier pyramids, the blocks were laid at an angle in the belief that this method gave greater stability to the building. As in the Bent Pyramid, the antechamber and burial chamber are roofed with very fine corbelled blocks.

Excavations by Dr Rainer Stadelmann of the German Archaeological Institute have revealed a large number of graffiti scribbled on pieces of limestone casing by the builders of the Red Pyramid. The most interesting thing about these inscriptions is that they are dated. One, from a corner of the pyramid, implies that Sneferu began to build it in the 30th year of his reign. Another, which had originally been placed about 30 courses of stone higher up, was dated four years

later. From these marks, it has been possible to deduce the length of time it took to build a pyramid, in this case about twenty years.

The mortuary temple was on the east side of the Red Pyramid and the ground plan has been reconstructed. Enough remained to make possible a reconstruction on paper of the temple's original appearance. It seems to have been much larger than the mortuary temples of the Meidum and Bent Pyramids, and was a worthy forerunner of the even larger Great Pyramid of Khufu at Giza. Lying in the mortuary temple is the reconstructed pyramidion, or solid limestone capstone, that once topped the pyramid. ◆

▼ *The Red Pyramid is second only in base size to the Great Pyramid of Khufu but is about 15m (49ft) lower because of its more gentle angle.*

How the Pyramids were Built

The first step in building a pyramid was to choose a suitable site. This had to be on the west side of the Nile because the west was where the sun set and where the dead were thought to enter the Underworld. The pyramid also needed to be situated on high ground, away from the danger of flooding at the time of the Nile's inundation. However, it could not be too far away from the bank because the river would be used to transport blocks of fine-quality limestone for the outer casing from Tura, on the other side of the Nile. The site chosen would be at a point on the desert plateau that would provide a firm rock base capable of supporting the great weight of the pyramid without any risk of cracking. It would also need to be within easy reach of the capital, so that the king could go to inspect the building work whenever he wished.

Site preparation

No plans for a pyramid exist, although there are extant plans of tombs in the Valley of the Kings. However, the building of a pyramid was not a haphazard affair and the measurements were accurate to a high degree. The workers had first to prepare a firm foundation by removing the loose sand from the rock. Then the rock base had to be made absolutely flat. The workers may have done this by building low mud walls all round the base and cutting channels in a grid pattern over the surface. Then they would have filled the channels with water and marked the level it reached. After the water had drained away, protruding rock would have been cut back to the level indicated, and any depressions filled with stones to make a perfectly level surface.

Each side of the pyramid had to face one of the cardinal points. The builders probably established true north first and worked out the other directions from that. They may have found true north by taking a sighting on a particular star in the northern sky. They would then observe the rising and setting of the star and mark its appearance and disappearance on an artificial horizon. By bisecting the angle thus made, they would obtain a north-south line. They had instruments for drawing right angles, so they would then have been able to find east and west. Next, they had to make the base perfectly square, with all four sides exactly the same length and the corners perfect right angles.

The workforce

Herodotus claimed that the Great Pyramid was built using slave labour, with 100,000 men at a time working in three-monthly shifts, for a period of 20 years. The idea of slave labour is now discounted, and it is thought more likely that the work did not carry on throughout the year, but only during the three months or so of the inundation period, when the workforce could not be employed on the land.

▼ *An artist's impression of the construction of the Giza pyramids, based on a drawing of Heinrich Leutemann. Groups of workers haul the massive blocks into position.*

Raising the blocks

Sometimes a rocky outcrop was used as the core of the pyramid to save work. The inner chambers and passages would have been constructed independently and the actual pyramid built around them. Some of the royal pyramid builders seem to have changed their minds about their preferred location of the burial chamber. The inner pyramid would then be built of limestone cut from the desert plateau. When the main structure was finished, the pyramid was completed by encasing it in blocks of finely cut and dressed limestone from Tura. Sometimes granite was used for the lower courses.

The precise method of raising the pyramid is not known. Pulleys were apparently not invented until Roman times. However, the Greek historian Herodotus tells of levers being used to raise the blocks from one level to the next. It has also been suggested that workers operating in teams used ramps to haul the blocks into position. As the pyramid grew in size so the ramp would have been raised to enable the workers to reach the next level. The main problem with this is that the ramp would eventually have been as huge as the pyramid itself and would have reached an immense distance into the desert. No trace of such a structure has definitely been identified at any of the various pyramid sites. Another idea is that the ramp wound around the pyramid and was dismantled when the pyramid was completed. Construction methods are still hotly debated. ◆

▲ *Scene from a stela of Ahmose I commemorating the reopening of the quarries at Maasara in his 22nd year, showing oxen hauling a stone block.*

▼ *The production of mudbricks, as depicted in the tomb of Rekhmire at Thebes. Mudbrick remains an important building material in Egypt today.*

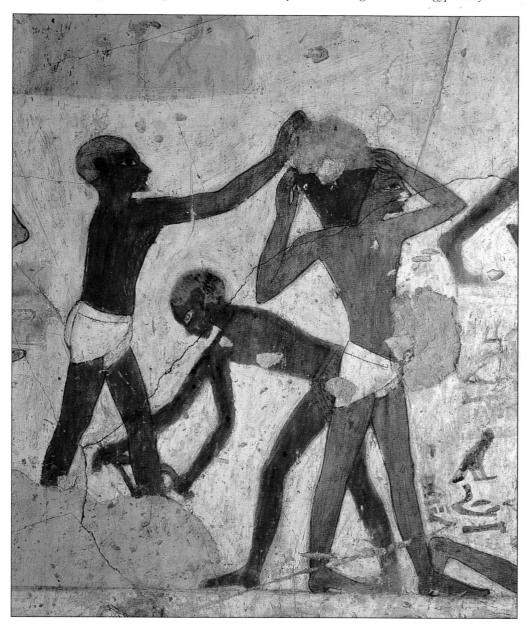

The Pyramid Texts

The Pyramid Texts are a collection of spells that were meant to ensure the resurrection of the king and his union with the gods in the sky. The texts appear for the first time covering the walls of the burial chamber and adjoining rooms in the pyramid of the last king of the Fifth Dynasty, Unas (c.2375–c.2345 BC), which was erected near the Step Pyramid of Djoser at Saqqara. Similar collections are found in the burial suites of the Sixth Dynasty kings Teti (c.2345–c.2323 BC), Pepi I (c.2321–c.2287 BC), Merenre (c.2287–c.2278 BC) and Pepi II (c.2278–c.2184 BC).

These texts are our best source of information about religious belief in the Old Kingdom. Not only do they shed light on beliefs concerning the king's Afterlife, but they also make many references to ancient Egyptian mythology. One text from the passageway leading to Unas' burial chamber reads:

This Unas comes to you, O Nut,
This Unas comes to you, O Nut,
He has consigned his father to
   the earth,
He has left Horus behind him.
Grown are his falcon wings,
Plumes of the holy hawk;
His ba has brought him
His magic has equipped him.

Nut, the sky goddess, welcomes Unas to the Afterlife with the words:

Make your seat in heaven,
Among the stars in heaven.

Another spell, this time from the ante-chamber, calls on the gods for assistance. Shu, the god of air, is asked to lift the king up, while Nut bends down to take his hand. The king is also thought to climb up to the sky on a ladder:

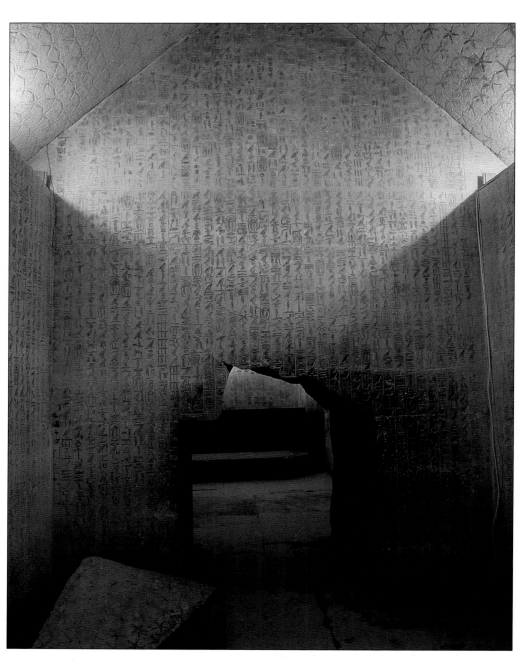

Hail, daughter of Anubis, above the
   hatches of heaven,
Comrade of Thoth, above the
   ladder's rails,
Open Unas' path, let Unas pass!

Sometimes the king calls on a celestial ferryman, in fact the ferryman of the gods, to take him across the water that was thought to separate earth and sky:

▲ *The first Pyramid Texts were found in the burial chamber of Unas. In these, he climbs a ladder to be united with his father Re-Atum.*

Awake in peace...
Sky's ferryman, in peace,
Nut's ferryman, in peace,
Ferryman of gods, in peace!
Unas has come to you
That you may ferry him in this boat
   in which you ferry the gods.

Should the ferryman refuse, a solution to the problem could be found in the form of Thoth, the god of wisdom, who is often represented as an ibis:

If you fail to ferry Unas,
He will leap and sit on the wing
  of Thoth,
Then he will ferry Unas to that side!

Most of all, the king desires to spend eternity united with his father, Re, the sun god:

Re-Atum, your son comes to you,
Unas comes to you,
Raise him to you, hold him in
  your arms,
He is your son, of your body,
  forever!

Although the texts are found in pyramids only towards the end of the Old Kingdom, the material embodied in them may be much older. An indication of this can be seen in a text of King Teti, which seems to make reference to a time when burials were much simpler:

Oho! Oho! Rise up, O Teti!
Take your head,
Collect your bones,
Gather your limbs,
Shake the earth from your flesh!

The same text implies that commoners are excluded from heaven, which is the prerogative of kings:

Stand at the gates which bar
  the common people!
The gatekeeper comes out to you,

▶ *The ceilings of royal burial chambers were decorated with stars as the king, on death, hoped to take his place in heaven among the 'imperishable stars'.*

He grasps your hand, takes you into
  heaven, to your father Geb.
He rejoices at your coming,
Gives you his hands,
Kisses you, caresses you,
Sets you before the spirits, the
  imperishable stars.

Teti is also seen sailing with the sun god, a theme that first occurs in the Pyramid of Unas:

Teti will take his pure seat in the
  bow of Re's barque:
The sailors who row Re, they shall
  row Teti!
The sailors who convey Re about
  lightland,
They shall convey Teti about
  lightland!

In the burial chamber of Pepi I there are several references to the myth of Osiris, with whom Pepi is united in the Afterlife. Pepi is said to be:

…the Great One…fallen on his side,
He who…in Nedyt was cast down.

This is an allusion to the murder of Osiris by his jealous brother, Seth. Pepi, like Osiris, hopes to be raised from the dead and to become Orion.

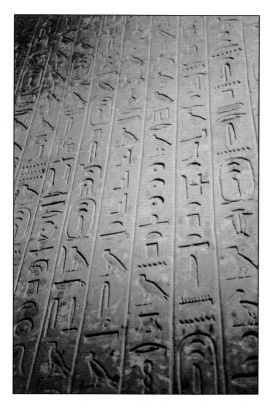

▲ *Texts from the tomb of Teti describe how he takes his seat in the sun god's boat and sails with him across the sky. Another text tells how his father Geb welcomes him into heaven.*

Your hand is grasped by Re,
Your head is raised (by all
  the gods)
Lo, he has come as Orion,
Lo, Osiris has come as Orion…

You shall live!
You shall rise with Orion in the
  eastern sky,
You shall set with Orion in the
  western sky. ◆

The Abusir Necropolis

Several of the kings of the Fifth Dynasty (c.2494–c.2345 BC) built their pyramids at Abusir, a name that is ultimately derived from Per Wsir, which means 'Place of Osiris'. The pyramids here are not as large as those of the Fourth Dynasty kings, and it has been suggested that this smaller size reflects a corresponding decline in royal power. That this might not be so is perhaps borne out by the fact that the quality of the materials used and the standard of much of the workmanship remains high. When in 1902–8 the German Egyptologist Ludwig Borschardt excavated the pyramid complex of Sahure (c.2487–c.2475 BC), the second king of the Fifth Dynasty, he found a great number of painted, delicately carved reliefs.

Pyramid complex of Sahure

Although Sahure's complex is the best preserved of those at Abusir, the pyramid itself is in a dilapidated condition. Once the outer casing had been removed, the inner core deteriorated into a heap of rubble. The core had been formed of five or six steps built with rough blocks of local limestone, held together with mud mortar. Borschardt found evidence for a wide 'construction gap' on the northern side of the pyramid, which gave the builders room to work

on the inner chambers while the construction of the pyramid itself went on around them. Granite had been used to line parts of the passageway leading to the burial chamber and for the portcullis that blocked the first section. The burial chamber itself was built entirely of Tura limestone and was roofed with three layers of huge limestone blocks placed at an angle.

Sahure's valley temple was on the edge of the Abusir Lake, from where a ramp led to a portico. The roof of this building was decorated with gold stars on a blue ground and supported by eight granite columns with palmiform capitals. Granite had also been used for the lower part of the walls and black basalt for the floor.

▲ *Remains of the pyramid of the 5th Dynasty king Sahure, at Abusir, where the pyramids are much smaller than those at Giza.*

The upper walls were of limestone carved with reliefs showing the king as a sphinx trampling his enemies.

The causeway was also decorated in relief and included scenes showing the gods leading prisoners representing Egypt's enemies – Asiatics and Libyans. These set a trend that was followed until the end of the Pharaonic Period.

The mortuary temple is the most interesting part of Sahure's complex, and became a model for those of later kings. It consists of five parts: entrance hall, open court, five niches for statues, storerooms and a sanctuary. The open court was paved with basalt and surrounded by a cloister decorated with scenes of the king receiving booty and smiting his enemies. Granite columns and palm-frond capitals again supported the starry roof. Running around the outside of the court was a wide corridor decorated with an entirely different type of relief. On the northern side the king was shown fishing and fowling in the

◄ *Travertine/calcite altar from Niuserre's sun temple at Abu Gurab. The shape has been interpreted as a huge hieroglyph meaning 'May Re be satisfied'.*

▶ *Following earlier tradition, the great officials of the 5th Dynasty were buried near their royal masters. The tomb of Ptahshepses, shown here, is one of the most splendid.*

marshes, and on the southern side he was depicted hunting with his courtiers and his successor, Neferirkare (c.2475–c.2455 BC). These reliefs are today in the Berlin Museum.

Neferirkare planned a pyramid complex at Abusir. His pyramid was to have been bigger than that of his predecessor, but it was never finished. Although the mortuary temple seems to have been hurriedly completed in mudbrick, only the foundations of the causeway and valley temple had been finished. When his son, Niuserre (c.2445–c.2421 BC), became king, he removed these elements from his father's complex and incorporated them into his own.

Tomb of Ptahshepses

Close to the pyramid of Sahure is the magnificent tomb of his vizier, Ptahshepses. The complex includes a portico, with the earliest-known example of columns with lotus-bud capitals, an offering room with statue niches, a huge courtyard surrounded with square pillars and a burial chamber with the fine granite sarcophagus still in situ.

Sun temples

Near to their pyramids, the kings of the Fifth Dynasty built sun temples to honour Re, the Heliopolitan sun god, at Abu Gurab. The Abusir Papyri and other documents mention six, although only two have been found so far, those of Userkaf (c.2494–c.2487 BC) and Niuserre. Userkaf's was the first royal building in this part of the necropolis, his pyramid being at Saqqara, close to the Step Pyramid of King Djoser. The remains, such as they are, were excavated between 1954–7 by a team from the Swiss Institute in Cairo. Niuserre, who also built his own sun temple at the nearby site of Abu Gurab, added extensively to Userkaf's temple.

Niuserre's sun temple is in a much better state of preservation. Although not much remains on the site today, the German expedition of 1898–1902 found enough clues to make possible a reconstruction on paper. It seems that the sun temple was part of a larger complex with the same component parts as a pyramid complex, including a valley temple and connecting causeway. Like the pyramid complex, it may have had a

◀ *Calcite bowls from the court of Niuserre's sun temple, used in the purification of offerings.*

funerary function. The sun god was one of the chief gods of the Afterlife, and was also the main creator god. If the sun temple is considered to be part of the pyramid complex, there is no need to see the monuments of the kings of the Fifth Dynasty as being in any way inferior to those of the Fourth. ◆

The Abusir Papyri

Details of the cult of the dead king can be found in an archive called the Abusir Papyri. They date from the reign of King Djedkare (c.2414–c.2375 BC) and are mostly concerned with the administration of the mortuary cult of King Neferirkare (c.2475–c.2455 BC). They provide an insight into the duties of the priests involved in the daily ritual, as well as important festivals. They laid down which offerings were to be brought on given dates, supplied rotas for guard duty, and indicated the organization of the workforce. There are also inventories of temple furniture and ritual vessels, and sets of accounts of the temple's income and expenditure.

Mudbrick Pyramids

Some of the kings of the Middle Kingdom (c.2055–c.1650 BC) built mudbrick pyramids in the Faiyum Oasis. They do not exactly follow the Old Kingdom model, and display a number of unusual features.

The pyramid of Senusret II

Senusret II (c.1880–c.1874 BC) built his pyramid at el-Lahun, an important agricultural centre near the Middle Kingdom capital, close to where the Bahr Yusef leaves the Nile and enters the Faiyum. The pyramid was built around a core of limestone, over which a limestone framework was erected and filled with mudbrick. The upper part of the pyramid was entirely of mudbrick. The exterior was then cased in limestone, with the blocks of the bottom course set into a trench cut into the rock.

Senusret departed from usual practice by placing the entrance on the southern side of his pyramid instead of on the northern side. This may have been intended to outwit potential robbers but, if so, it failed. All that was left of Senusret's burial was a gold *uraeus*, the royal headdress in the protective form of a rearing cobra, and a few leg bones, presumably of the king.

Very little remains of the mortuary and valley temples or the causeway. Surrounding the pyramid were two walls, one of stone and one of mudbrick. Beyond the outer wall, trees had been planted in pits sunk into the rock and filled with earth. Inside the enclosure wall on the northern side of the pyramid was a row of eight mastaba tombs, at the eastern end of which was a small pyramid. It is not clear whether this was a subsidiary tomb connected with the king's own burial or whether it was intended for a queen. Between the enclosure walls on the southern side of the pyramid were four shaft tombs. One

▲ *A statue of Amenemhet III from his pyramid complex at Hawara. His burial chamber was cut from a single block of quartzite.*

▼ *The first of the mudbrick pyramids belonged to Senusret II who built his final resting place at el-Lahun in the Faiyum.*

▶ *Amenemhet III planned to be buried at Dahshur but seems to have abandoned the idea when the pyramid began to show signs of structural stress. He built a second pyramid at Hawara.*

of these was the burial place of Princess Sithathoriunet, and contained a collection of jewellery, which was part of her funerary equipment.

The Labyrinth

Amenemhat III (c.1855–c.1808 BC), famous for his land reclamation schemes, sited one of his pyramids at Hawara in the Faiyum. Like that of Senusret II, it was built of mudbrick and cased in limestone. It was almost 60m (197ft) tall and was the last large pyramid to be built in Egypt. On the southern side of the pyramid was a vast structure known to Herodotus and other classical authors as the Labyrinth. It covered an area of 6 hectares (15 acres) and had 12 covered courts, six in a row facing north and six

▼ *Carved limestone crocodiles representing the god Sobek once adorned the 'Labyrinth', in fact the mortuary temple of the Hawara pyramid.*

facing south, with the gates of the one range exactly fronting the gates of the other, with a continuous wall around the outside of the whole. Inside, the building was of two storeys and contained 3,000 rooms, of which half were underground with the other half directly above them.

Herodotus wrote that he was not allowed to see the underground rooms because they contained the tombs of the kings who built the Labyrinth and also the tombs of crocodiles, which were worshipped in the Faiyum. However, he was allowed to see the rest and could hardly believe his eyes as he wandered

through this maze of rooms, galleries and courtyards. None of this remains today, and even when Flinders Petrie excavated the site in 1888–9 he could recognize very few details of this most unusual of mortuary temples. ◆

The workers' town of Kahun

Not far from Senusret's valley temple was the town of Kahun, where the workers on the pyramid lived. This site was exhaustively excavated by Flinders Petrie, who discovered a vast number of domestic objects in the form of pottery, loom weights, mirrors, combs, stone and faience vases for perfumed oils and ointments, pots of kohl used as eye-liner, rush baskets of various shapes and sizes, rush sandals, carpenters' tools, fish hooks, agricultural implements and toys. There was even a rat trap. Different types of houses and their interior decoration also came to light. A large number of documents were found, including wills and some extremely interesting gynaecological and veterinary papyri. From these, it has been possible to build up a full picture of life in this town, which was the first of the pyramid workers' towns to be discovered and excavated.

Royal Jewellery of the Twelfth Dynasty

Several of the daughters of the kings of the Middle Kingdom (c.2055–c.1650 BC) were buried in shaft graves near to their father's pyramid. Some of the shafts contained sumptuous collections of diadems, bracelets, pectorals and collars. Middle Kingdom jewellery is considered to be some of the most exquisite ever made, either in ancient Egypt or elsewhere. Both in terms of inspiration and craftsmanship it is unparalleled.

Jewellery of Princess Sithathoriunet

When Flinders Petrie and Guy Brunton explored the shaft tomb of Princess Sithathoriunet in 1914, they found little apart from her red granite sarcophagus and a set of canopic jars, the vessels which accompanied each burial to house the internal organs. Then they discovered a niche in the wall that had been plastered over. Inside were five boxes containing Sithathoriunet's jewellery, a mirror, razors and pots for cosmetics.

▶ *The silver mirror of Sithathoriunet is a jewellery masterpiece. It is supported by a head of Hathor mounted on an obsidian handle.*

The prize piece in this collection is a diadem in the form of a broad band of gold decorated with the *uraeus* (the royal cobra) and rosettes. It also has two gold plumes and three sets of detachable gold streamers. It would have been worn on top of a wig made up of dozens of long braids held in little gold clasps. The cobra's head is made of lapis lazuli and the eyes of garnets set in gold rims. The rosettes are inlaid with lapis, carnelian and green faience in imitation of feldspar and turquoise. The diadem is now on display in the Cairo Museum.

There are also two pectorals (chest ornaments) in the collection. One has the name of the princess's father, Senusret II (c.1880–c.1874 BC), worked into the design and the other the name of her nephew, Amenemhat III (c.1855–c.1808 BC), during whose reign she died.

▲ *The stunning gold diadem of Sithathoriunet was found in her tomb in the funerary complex of Senusret II.*

The toilet articles are as beautiful as the jewellery. Among them are some elegant black vases for perfumed oils and ointments, but the masterpiece is the mirror. This consists of a thick silver disc surmounting a handle of obsidian in the form of an open papyrus plant. Below the umbel, which is covered in electrum (an alloy of silver and gold) is the head of Hathor, goddess of sexual love, worked in gold with eyes of lapis lazuli. The head has Hathor's characteristic cow's ears, symbolizing her nurturing role: she was worshipped as a universal mother goddess, but was particularly associated with kings. The mirror is double-faced, both sides being identical. Around the neck are four rings inlaid with carnelian, stone and faience, as is the pointed corolla of the base. The triangular shape of the papyrus stem is outlined in granulation work. This mirror would have ensured that the princess, whose name included that of Hathor, putting her under the protection of the goddess, enjoyed her gifts of eternal youth and beauty in the Afterlife.

Jewellery of Princess Neferuptah

A further collection of jewellery and toilet articles was discovered in 1956 at Hawara in the tomb of Princess Neferuptah, possibly a daughter of Amenemhat III. One of the most impressive pieces is a broad collar composed of six bands of tubular beads made of feldspar and carnelian, with little gold beads between them. Below this is a border of golden droplets inlaid with feldspar heads in repoussé work. The collar is balanced by a counterpoise consisting of a miniature falcon head above a series of narrow bands of beads, which match the main part of the collar. Matching pairs of bracelets and anklets complete the set.

Jewellery of Princess Meret

Some of the Middle Kingdom kings built mudbrick tombs at Dahshur. Princess Meret, daughter of Senusret III (c.1874–c.1855 BC), was buried close to his pyramid there. Two finely wrought pectorals were among the funerary equipment found in her tomb. They are made in the form of shrines. Inside at the top, Nekhbet the vulture goddess, protector of kings, hovers with outspread wings above the image of the king trampling his enemies. One pectoral includes the name of her father and the other that of Amenemhat III, her brother.

▲ *A beautiful pectoral found in Princess Meret's tomb at Dahshur shows her father Senusret III as a griffin trampling his foes.*

▲ *Princess Neferuptah's collection included matching sets of bracelets and anklets. They were made of gold, carnelian and feldspar.*

Jewellery of Princess Sathathor

Princess Sathathor was also buried at Dahshur, close to the pyramid of Senusret III whose sister, and possibly wife, she was. Her jewellery includes a pectoral in the form of a shrine, with the name of her father, Senusret II, inscribed inside it. This is protected on each side by two striped falcons wearing the Double Crown of Upper and Lower Egypt.

Another delightful piece is a belt of gold cowrie shells and tiny beads. The clasp is formed of two half cowrie shells, which slide together along grooves to make a whole as they fasten the belt. ◆

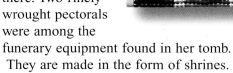

◀ *The intact tomb of Princess Neferuptah, found under a ruined mudbrick pyramid at Hawara, revealed another rich collection of jewellery. The princess was found wearing this collar.*

The Pyramids of the Kushite Kings

From the beginning of the New Kingdom (c.1550–c.1069 BC), kings abandoned the practice of burial within a pyramid and opted instead for a tomb in the Valley of the Kings in Western Thebes. The tradition of pyramid burial was, however, revived by the Kushite kings of the Twenty-fifth Dynasty, whose capital was at Napata in Upper Nubia. Egyptian control of Nubia had been lost after the end of the New Kingdom, and Nubia had developed as a separate kingdom. During the same period, several independent rulers, each powerful in his own district, had governed Egypt. The Kushite king, Piy (c.747–c.716 BC), marched north around 728 BC and brought the whole of Egypt under his control. His success was recorded on a great stela originally set up in the temple at Gebel Barkal and now in the Cairo Museum.

Burials at el-Kurru

The Kushite rulers regarded themselves as the true successors of the great Egyptian kings and emulated their activities in many ways, including that of building pyramids. Piy, his father, and several of his successors were buried in pyramids at el-Kurru. The style of these was rather different from the traditional structures, however. They were much more modest in size and had steeply sloping walls. Like the early Egyptian tombs, they seem to have evolved from

▲ *From the time of Taharqo, the Kushite kings were buried at Nuri in large elaborate tombs, which reflected Egyptian royal burial places.*

mastabas. However, they appear to have been modelled on small 'private' pyramids, known from the craftsmen's village at Deir el-Medina, rather than on the vast royal structures from the height of the Pyramid Age. Apart from the kings' tombs, 14 queens were also buried in pyramids at el-Kurru.

Piy and his immediate successors, Shabaqo (c.716–c.702 BC) and Shabitqo (c.702–690 BC) were buried on beds within the tomb chamber. But from the time of Taharqo (690–664 BC), the kings adopted the Egyptian practice of using coffins and sarcophagi. Mummification was practised and the grave goods included traditional *shabti* figures, small statuettes of servants who would do whatever work was necessary in the

◀ *Pyramids of the kings and queens of Meroe in the North Cemetery. They were built on a ridge in imitation of Egyptian pyramids.*

▶ Shabtis *of Taharqo from his pyramid at Nuri. They were exceptionally large and made of serpentine, calcite and black granite. The features of the king indicate that he was Nubian, and the texts reflect the interest of the Kushite kings in earlier periods.*

▲ *One of Taharqo's shabtis. Kushite kings were buried in Egyptian-style coffins and sarcophagi. Bodies were mummified and provided with shabtis.*

Afterlife. One distinguishing feature was the continuation of the Kushite practice of horse burials. The royal chariot horses were apparently sacrificed, decapitated and buried standing in pits in a special cemetery near the pyramids of el-Kurru.

Nuri

From the time of Taharqo, members of the Kushite royal family were buried at Nuri. Here the pyramids were much larger than those at el-Kurru and the chapels were decorated with reliefs. A stela built into the pyramid showed the king, in Egyptian fashion, before the gods. Taharqo's pyramid was the largest of all and was built in two stages, the inner pyramid having been encased with limestone. The subterranean rooms were also more elaborate than in any other of the Nuri tombs. The entrance was on the eastern side and led eventually to a doorway with a moulded frame and cavetto (concave) cornice. From there a tunnel led to an antechamber with a barrel-vaulted ceiling. In the burial chamber, there were six great pillars cut from the rock. These divided the room into three, each part having a barrel-vaulted ceiling. A shallow pit had been cut into the floor to take the sarcophagus, and four niches were incorporated into the walls. Surrounding the burial chamber was a 'moat' reached by a flight of steps.

The last royal burial at Nuri took place at the end of the fourth century BC. From this time, the city of Meroe in the Sudan became important, and the kings built their pyramids there. Meroe remained the royal cemetery for much of the next 600 years, until the disintegration of the kingdom in around AD 350. ◆

◀ *Taharqo, the most famous of the Kushite kings, dressed as a pharaoh. He kneels before the falcon god, Hemen, who holds a cobra in his talons. The deity is a Nubian version of the Egyptian god Horus.*

The Pyramids of Giza

Giza was the most important royal necropolis of the Fourth Dynasty (c.2613–c.2494 BC), and it is where the most famous of all the pyramids were built. Although today the three main pyramids have been almost engulfed by the sprawling suburb of Giza, they still retain their awe-inspiring majesty. These colossal monuments are not the only sights worth seeing at Giza. They are surrounded by the smaller pyramids of queens and princesses, and the mastaba tombs of high officials, several of which can now be visited. Recent excavation has also revealed a cemetery where dwarfs were buried. In life, these men were highly respected and held important posts, and in death they were considered to be worthy of a tomb close to their royal master.

A further exciting find in recent years has been the discovery of the town inhabited by the workers who built the pyramids. It came to light during work on the construction of a sewage system for the villages near to the Great Pyramid. An extensive settlement site dating from the Old Kingdom (c.2686–c.2181 BC) was discovered near the valley temple of Khufu. Hundreds of objects relating to the daily life of the workers and their families have been found here, and the associated cemetery has also been discovered.

◀ *Visited by Herodotus in the mid-5th century BC, and one of the Wonders of the Ancient World, the Giza pyramids are now closed in rotation as a means of conservation.*

The Great Pyramids

The most famous of all the landmarks of present-day Egypt, and one of the Wonders of the Ancient World, the Giza pyramids were the burial places of the Fourth Dynasty kings, Khufu, Khafre and Menkaure. Each pyramid was part of a larger complex consisting of a mortuary temple, a causeway, a valley temple and subsidiary pyramids, while the pyramid of Khufu is surrounded by five boat pits. The pyramids were robbed in antiquity, but the contents of the concealed tomb of Queen Hetepheres, the mother of Khufu, give some idea of the richness of the burials of the kings. The pyramid complexes are surrounded by 'streets' of mastaba tombs belonging to the officials who served as administrators or were in charge of the funerary cults of the deceased kings. Current excavation is beginning to shed light on the lives and deaths of the workers who toiled to build the memorials to the ancient kings. ◆

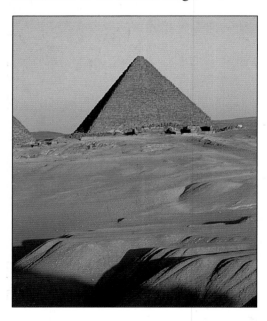

▲ *The Great Pyramid of Khufu was the largest of the three pyramids at Giza. It appears smaller than that of Khafre, which was built on higher ground.*

Pyramid of Khafre

Storage Rooms

Pyramid of Menkaure

Mortuary Templ

Queens' Pyramids

Causeway

N

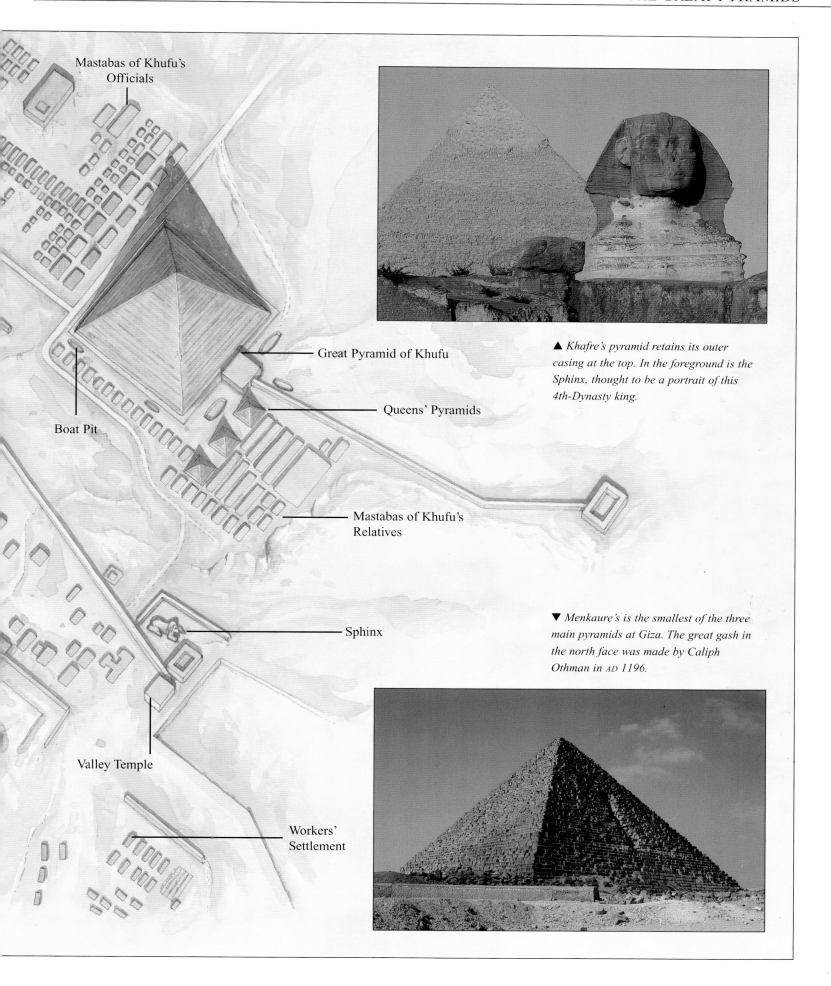

Mastabas of Khufu's
Officials

Boat Pit

Great Pyramid of Khufu

Queens' Pyramids

Mastabas of Khufu's
Relatives

Sphinx

Valley Temple

Workers'
Settlement

▲ *Khafre's pyramid retains its outer casing at the top. In the foreground is the Sphinx, thought to be a portrait of this 4th-Dynasty king.*

▼ *Menkaure's is the smallest of the three main pyramids at Giza. The great gash in the north face was made by Caliph Othman in AD 1196.*

The Great Pyramid of Khufu

The Great Pyramid of the Fourth Dynasty king Khufu (c.2589–c.2566 BC) is the largest of all the pyramids. It was originally 140m (460ft) tall but is now 3m (10ft) less. At the base, the sides each measured 140m (460ft), but are now only 127m (417ft) because the pyramid has been stripped of its limestone casing. Some of this was removed in antiquity, but much was also taken in the ninth century AD when the caliphs built the city of Cairo. Amelia Edwards thought this gave the pyramid an unfinished look, as if the workmen 'were coming back tomorrow morning'. It is estimated that about 2,300,000 blocks, each weighing an average of 2.3 tons (although some weigh much more) went into the building of the pyramid.

The original entrance is on the north face and is 15m (49ft) above ground level, surmounted by a double vault. The lower entrance, used by tourists today, was made in the ninth century AD when an entry was forced on the orders of Caliph Mamun.

Inside the Great Pyramid

There are at least three chambers inside the pyramid. From the entrance, a corridor leads downwards for 18m (60ft) and then divides. One branch leads on down to an underground chamber, which was left unfinished. The other climbs up towards the Grand Gallery, where it again divides. A horizontal tunnel leads to a second chamber, misleadingly known as the Queen's Chamber, while another tunnel winds precipitously to connect with the descending corridor.

The Grand Gallery is corbelled in the manner of Sneferu's pyramids and is a wonderful example of craftsmanship and precision. An antechamber once blocked by three granite slabs leads from it into the King's Chamber, the walls of which are lined with granite. The sarcophagus is plain and uninscribed. It has been suggested that the two chambers lower

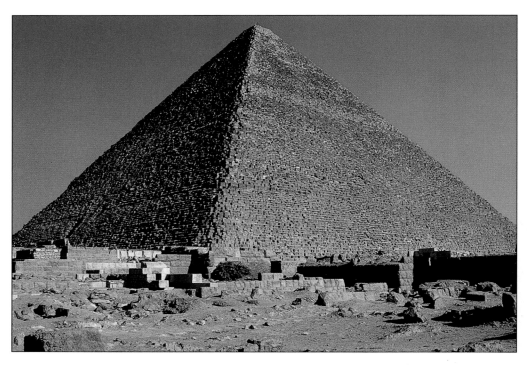

▲ *The Great Pyramid at Giza, largest of all the pyramids, was stripped of its casing of white limestone in antiquity and during the 9th century.*

down the pyramid were intended as burial chambers, but first one and then the other was found to be too small to house the large granite sarcophagus, so it became necessary to alter the plans. This would have been possible, as the internal chambers were constructed while the main work of building the pyramid went on around them. The King's Chamber is roofed with nine granite slabs weighing about 400 tons. Above are five weight-relieving chambers, one above the other, designed to carry the enormous weight of the rest of the pyramid.

Two small shafts, once thought to be for ventilation, lead north and south from the burial chamber to the outside. Recent research by the German Archaeological Institute has shown that they are nothing to do with the circulation of air, but had a purely ritual use. They were to provide a direct route to heaven for the soul of the king. According to the same

▲ *The Grand Gallery leads from the ascending corridor to the burial chamber of Khufu. The walls are 8.5m (28ft) high and 47m (154ft) long and are corbelled, each layer of limestone blocks projecting about 6cm (2½in) beyond the one on which it rests.*

◄ The only surviving image of Khufu, builder of the Great Pyramid, this tiny limestone statuette is in the Egyptian Museum, Cairo. Although the fugure is tiny, just 7.5cm (3in) tall, the face is full of character.

causeway and mortuary temple. The mortuary temple was much bigger than those of the Meidum and Dahshur pyramids. It had a colonnade surrounding a large court paved with basalt. The limestone walls had carved reliefs. According to Herodotus, the causeway was also decorated with reliefs, and some pieces have now come to light to support his statement. The valley temple has almost completely disappeared, although some basalt paving blocks found in 1990 by Dr Zahi Hawass, Director-General of the Giza Pyramids and Saqqara, may once have belonged to it.

On the south side of the pyramid, there were three small pyramids belonging to the queens Henutsen, Meritetis and Hetepheres, Khufu's mother. Khufu's own (tiny) secondary pyramid was found in 1991 by Zahi Hawass. The complex is completed by five boat pits, which either represented or contained boats to enable the deceased king, in his identification with the sun god, to make his celestial voyages. To the east of the complex lie the mastabas of his relatives, while those of his officials are to the west. ◆

Images of Khufu

If there were ever any statues of Khufu in the temple complex they have vanished without trace. The only surviving image of this king is a tiny statuette found by Flinders Petrie at Abydos and now in the Cairo Museum. In fact Khufu's only firm link with the pyramid is his cartouche in the topmost of the relieving chambers above the burial chamber.

study, the three internal chambers also had a ritual purpose and the team would dispute the suggestion that they represent changes in plan.

The Queen's Chamber also has a similar pair of shafts, which were partly explored when the pyramid was closed for conservation in 1992. A tiny robot penetrated 65m (213ft) into the pyramid before it was stopped by a 'door' with two copper handles. It is hoped that exploration will continue in the near future. A new gilded limestone capstone was made to celebrate the turning of the millennium.

The pyramid complex

Although little remains today, the pyramid once possessed a valley temple,

▶ This plan of the interior of the Great Pyramid by Benoit de Maillet was published in 1735 before the descending corridor had been fully explored.

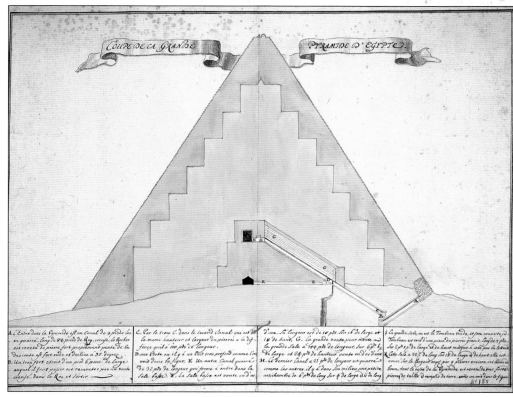

The Pyramid of Khafre

The pyramid complex of Khafre is the most complete of all the Giza pyramids. Because it was built on slightly higher ground and rises at a sharper angle, the pyramid itself appears to be larger than Khufu's, although it is actually second in size. Near the top it still retains some of its original casing stones. The other component parts of the complex, especially the valley temple, are also much more in evidence here.

There are two entrances to the pyramid on the north side, of which the lower one is used by tourists today. This leads to a passage that first descends and then rises, before running horizontally to the burial chamber, which is just below ground level. The Italian adventurer Giovanni Belzoni entered the burial chamber on 2 March 1818, as his inscription proclaims. Inside was an empty plain red granite sarcophagus, with no inscriptions.

In its heyday, the pyramid was served by a magnificent mortuary temple, 110m (360ft) long, with two pylons, a transverse vestibule and a rectangular hall, both embellished with columns. Then came a large court surrounded by a columned portico where there would

▲ *The pyramid of Khafre, which still retains part of its original high-quality Tura limestone casing. Khafre's funerary complex is the best preserved of the three at Giza.*

have been statues of the king. Behind this were five small chapels, storehouses and an inner sanctuary. Sadly, the temple has been used as a quarry over the centuries, and little of its ancient splendour can be seen today.

Khafre's valley temple

Although it has lost its roof, much remains of the causeway along which the king's body would have been brought from the valley temple. Khafre's magnificent valley temple is the best preserved of any that have come to light so far. It was discovered by Auguste Mariette in 1858, and is sometimes known as the Granite Temple because of

◄ *Khafre spared no expense on the construction of his valley temple. It is lined with huge blocks of polished Aswan granite and the floors are paved with alabaster from Hatnub.*

the huge blocks of polished red Aswan granite from which it was constructed. These enormous blocks were cut with astounding precision. Some have even been cut so that they turn corners. The floors are of polished alabaster.

In the T-shaped hall are emplacements for 23 statues of Khafre. These would have been illuminated by light entering through slits high up on the walls. Only the bases of most of these statues remain, but Mariette found one splendid complete version lying in a well in the vestibule. It is a little larger than life-size and is made of polished diorite from the quarries at Toshka in Nubia. Khafre is seated on the throne of the Two Lands. Behind him sits Horus, in the form of a falcon, with his wings folded protectively around the king's head.

The king's body would have been transported from the capital, Memphis, by boat. A quay has been discovered in front of the Sphinx temple, and it may have continued in front of the valley temple.

The site of the secondary pyramid has now been located to the east of the pyramid. Only the foundations of the superstructure remain, but when the underground section was explored one of the two passages was found to end in a niche that once contained the remains of a wooden shrine. This may have held a statue of the king; in some tomb scenes such a shrine housing a statue of the deceased is shown being dragged towards the tomb.

The Sphinx

Egypt's earliest colossal royal statue, the Sphinx, is also an integral part of Khafre's complex. In spite of some of the more bizarre theories recently put forward, most Egyptologists regard the Sphinx as a portrait statue of the king carved from an outcrop of rock that remained after the quarrying of limestone for the interior of the Great Pyramid. Rather than leaving it as something of a

◀ Twenty-three diorite statues of Khafre once graced his valley temple, although only this one, now in the Cairo Museum, survives intact. The king is protected by Horus, the falcon god.

▲ The famous Sphinx is carved from an outcrop of rock on the Giza Plateau. The lion's body symbolizes royal power, while the head is a portrait of Khafre. The features strongly resemble the diorite statue of the king.

blot on the landscape, it was transformed into this symbol of royal power, a lion's body with the head of the king.

During the New Kingdom (c.1550–c.1069 BC), the Sphinx was regarded as a manifestation of the sun god. Between its paws is the famous Dream Stela, an inscribed tablet that records the promise to the prince Tuthmosis, later Tuthmosis IV (c.1400–c.1390 BC), that the sun god would ensure that he became king of Egypt, though he was not the heir, should he clear away the sand that had drifted around the Sphinx and do any necessary repairs. Much conservation work has been done on the Sphinx in recent years, and the Sphinx Temple has also been restored. ◆

The Pyramid of Menkaure

The pyramid built by the Fourth Dynasty king Menkaure (c.2532– c.2503 BC) at Giza is only about half the size of those of his predecessors, Khufu and Khafre. The reason for this is unclear. Perhaps their building projects had put too great a strain on Egypt's resources. The builders may have been running out of suitable sites on the Giza Plateau. Or perhaps the kings now felt they needed to show more deference to the sun god, as witnessed by the small size of the royal burial places and the contemporary building of sun temples at Abusir during the Fifth Dynasty (c.2494–c.2345 BC).

Architectural innovations

Whatever the reason for its diminished size, the construction still used costly materials and the pyramid was designed with several original features. For instance, although it was partly cased in Tura limestone, 16 courses of red granite blocks were used for the lower section. Further, the entrance on the north side of the pyramid leads down to a horizontal chamber decorated with a false door motif. The lintel above the entrance to the horizontal corridor is carved in imitation of a rolled reed curtain. These are the first signs of decoration inside a pyramid since the time of Djoser (c.2667–c.2648 BC). Another new feature

was the complexity of the burial suite. A horizontal passage with three portcullises leads to an antechamber. From here, a second passage leads down to the burial chamber, lined with granite. When the English explorer Howard Vyse entered the pyramid in 1837 he found a sarcophagus carved with the 'palace façade' motif. It was removed for shipment to England, but was unfortunately lost in a storm at sea. A wooden coffin found in an upper

▼ *Despite being only about half the size of those of his predecessors, the pyramid of Menkaure was nonetheless built of costly materials, with granite being used for the casing of the lower part.*

▶ *Remains of the mortuary temple are still visible on the east side of the pyramid. Offerings to the king would have been brought here daily.*

chamber and containing the remains of a mummy was dispatched on a different ship and is now in the British Museum in London. The style of the coffin, however, dates it to the Twenty-sixth Dynasty, or Saite Period (664–525 BC), while the bones are from the Christian era. Attached to the burial chamber was a room divided into six small niches and probably intended as a store for the king's funerary goods.

Mortuary and valley temples

The remains of an unfinished complex mortuary temple can be seen against the eastern face of the pyramid. It consists of a vestibule leading from the causeway, a large open court, a pillared

◀ *The mudbrick valley temple was embellished with beautiful schist triads showing Menkaure protected by Hathor and various local deities.*

portico leading to the sanctuary and various ancillary rooms, presumably for cultic equipment. Building was started in limestone, although the intention appears to have been to case it in granite. Menkaure seems to have died before it was completed because the temple has been hurriedly finished off in mudbrick. The unfinished nature of the complex made its excavation by George Reisner in 1899 especially interesting, because it provided information about how the work had been done. When Reisner stripped away the mudbrick he could see that the limestone walls were being prepared to take the granite facing when the construction was interrupted. On the core blocks he found levelling lines, measurements and even the names of workers marked in red paint.

Not much remains of the limestone causeway. Like the valley temple, this is often said to have been completed by Menkaure's son, Shepseskaf (c.2503–c.2494 BC), but there is little evidence for this. The valley temple itself, even in Reisner's

time, lay beneath the sand. He found it by projecting the axis of the causeway from the entrance of the mortuary temple, and was fortunate enough to make some wonderful discoveries. First he found the pair-statue of Menkaure and his queen, Khamererenebty. He went on to find four more masterpieces of ancient Egyptian art, the famous triads showing Menkaure with the goddess Hathor and a local deity, which are now in the Cairo Museum.

Three small pyramids lie to the south of Menkaure's, one of which might have been intended as the king's subsidiary pyramid, later adapted to accommodate a queen. The body of a young woman was found in the central pyramid. ◆

Hathor

The king was thought to be the child of the gods. As the living king was regarded as Horus, his mother was often held to be Isis. However, in the triads that decorated Menkaure's valley temple, Hathor, whose name means 'House of Horus', plays that role. As a cow goddess she nurtures the king with her milk. In the Pyramid Texts the king is asked on his arrival in paradise, 'Are you Horus, the son of Osiris? Are you the god, the eldest one, the son of Hathor?'

Stories from Herodotus

In Book Two of *The Histories*, Herodotus related the stories of Cheops (Khufu c.2589–c.2566 BC) and Chephren (Khafre c.2558–c.2532 BC) as told to him by Egyptian priests during his visit to the pyramids in the mid-fifth century BC. He clearly regarded them as tyrants. In contrast, Mycerinus (Menkaure c.2532–c.2503 BC) was seen as a good king.

Oppressive rule

'Cheops…brought the country into all sorts of misery. He closed all the temples, then not content with excluding his subjects from the practice of their religion, compelled them without exception to labour as slaves for his own advantage. Some were forced to bring blocks of stone from the quarries in the Arabian hills to the Nile, where they were ferried across by others who hauled them to the Libyan hills. The work went on in three-monthly shifts, 100,000 men in a shift. It took ten years of this oppressive slave-labour to build the track along which the blocks were hauled, a work, in my opinion, of hardly less magnitude than the pyramid itself, for it is 5 furlongs [1km] in length, 60ft [18m] wide, 48ft [15m] high at its highest point, and constructed of polished stone blocks decorated with carvings of animals. To build it took, as I have said, ten years, including the underground sepulchral chambers on the hill where the pyramids stood: a cut was made from the Nile, so that the water from it turned the site of these into an island. To build the pyramid itself took 20 years: it is square at the base, its height equal to the length of each side; it is of polished stone blocks, beautifully fitted, none of the blocks being less than 30ft [9m] long. The method

employed was to build it in steps, or as some say, tiers or terraces. When the base was complete, the blocks for the first tier above it were lifted from the ground by contrivances made of short timbers; on this first tier there was another, which raised the blocks a stage higher, then yet another which raised them higher still. Each tier or storey had its set of levers, or it may be that they used the same one, which being easy to carry, they shifted up from stage to stage as soon as its load was dropped into place. Both methods are mentioned, so I give them both here. The finishing-off of the pyramid was begun at the top and

continued downwards, ending with the lowest parts nearest the ground. An inscription is cut upon it in Egyptian characters recording the amount spent on radishes, onions and leeks for the labourers. And I remember distinctly that the interpreter who read me the inscription said that the sum was 1,600 talents of silver...

But no crime was too great for Cheops: when he was short of money, he sent his daughter to a bawdy house with instructions to charge a certain sum, they did not tell me how much. This she actually did, adding to it a further transaction of her own; for with the intention of leaving something to be remembered by after her death, she asked each of her customers to give her a block of stone, and of these stones (the story goes) was built the middle pyramid of the three which stand in front of the great pyramid. It is a 150ft [45m] square.

Cheops reigned for 50 years according to the Egyptian's account, and was succeeded after his death by his brother Chephren. Chephren was no better than his predecessor: his rule was equally oppressive, and, like Cheops, he built a pyramid, but of a smaller size (I measured both of them myself)... The pyramid of Chephren lies close to that of Cheops; it is 40ft [12m] lower than the latter, but otherwise of the same dimensions; its lower course is of the coloured stone of Ethiopia.

Chephren reigned for 56 years, so the Egyptians reckon a period of 106 years, all told, when the temples were never opened for worship and the country reduced to the greatest possible misery...'

◄ *A bust said to be of the Greek historian Herodotus, who was one of the first travellers to Egypt to write of his experiences there.*

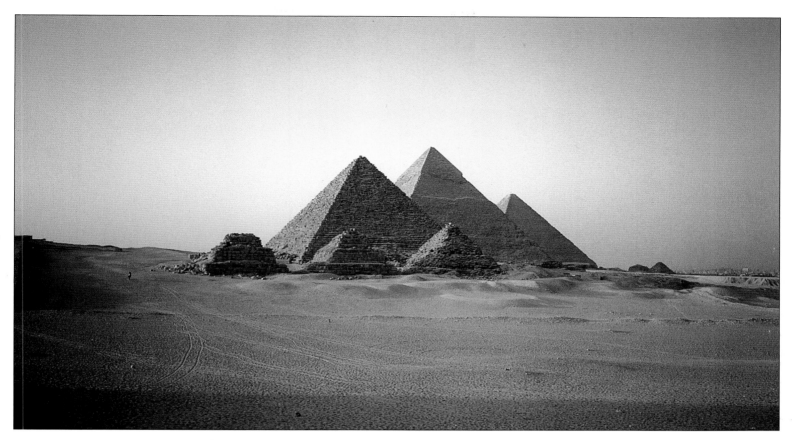

The reign of Menkaure

'The next king of Egypt to rule after Chephren was Mycerinus, the son of Cheops. Mycerinus, reversing his father's policy of which he did not approve, reopened all the temples and allowed his subjects, who had been brought into such abject slavery, to resume the practice of their religion and their normal work. Of all the kings who ruled in Egypt he had the greatest reputation for justice in the decision of legal causes, and for this the Egyptians give him higher praise than any other… He used to compensate out of his own property any man who was dissatisfied with the results of his suit, and so leave him nothing to complain of… Such were the generosity and mild rule of Mycerinus, when the first of his troubles fell upon him: his daughter, who was his only child, died. Wishing, in the excess of his grief at this calamity, to give his daughter a tomb which should be different from any other, he had a wooden cow made, hollow inside and plated on the outside with gold, to receive her body. The cow was not buried, but was still to be seen in my day at Sais, standing in a richly decorated chamber of the royal palace; incense of all kinds is burnt before it every day, and at night a lamp is always kept lighted in the room. Close by in another chamber, the priests told me, are some statues, which represent the concubines of Mycerinus: there are, indeed, 20 or so naked wooden figures of great size in this chamber, but as to whom they represent I can only pass on such information as was given to me.

There is another, and quite different, story told about the cow and the statues; according to this, Mycerinus conceived a passion for his daughter and violated her, and distress at the outrage drove her to hang herself: she was entombed in the cow, and her mother cut off the hands of the servants who had allowed the king access to her. The statues represent the servants, and like their living originals, have no hands. Personally I think this story is nonsense, especially in its explanation of the servants' missing hands; I could see for myself that they had simply dropped off through age. They are still there, plainly visible, lying on the ground at the statues' feet…

After the death of his daughter, a second calamity fell upon Mycerinus: he received an oracle from Buto to the

▲ *Herodotus visited the pyramids in the mid-5th century BC and was given his information by the priests who looked after the site.*

effect he was destined to live for only six more years and to die within the seventh. He sent back an angry message to the shrine, and reproached the god with the injustice of allowing a man so pious as himself to die so soon, when his father and uncle, who had closed the temples, forgotten the gods, and afflicted their fellow men, had lived to a good old age. In answer to this there was another message from the oracle, which declared that his life was being shortened precisely because he had not done what he ought to have done…Mycerinus, convinced by this that his doom was sealed, had innumerable lamps made, by the light of which he set himself every evening to drink and be merry, and never ceased by day or night from the pursuit of pleasure, travelling about from place to place amongst the pools and woodlands…His object in this was by turning night into day to extend the six remaining years of his life into twelve, and so convict the oracle of falsehood.' ◆

The Tomb of Hetepheres

Queen Hetepheres was the wife of Sneferu (c.2613–c.2589 BC) and the mother of Khufu (c.2589–c.2566 BC). It seems likely that she was originally buried at Dahshur, near her husband, but that her tomb was violated soon after she was laid to rest. Perhaps because of this, her reburial was ordered and a shaft grave assigned to her on the east side of Khufu's Great Pyramid, near the three small pyramids, the northernmost of which is also thought to be hers. The shaft tomb was discovered in 1925 by the staff photographer of the Harvard-Boston expedition led by George Reisner. It was found to contain some beautiful gilded wooden furniture, which is now displayed in a new gallery in the Cairo Museum.

Hetepheres' furniture

The furniture includes a large portable canopy and a box for the curtains that went with it. Both are inscribed with the name of Hetepheres' husband, and the rest of the furniture dates to his reign. One of the best pieces is a beautifully crafted, gilded wooden sedan chair, a mode of transport commonly seen in the tombs of high-ranking officials of the Old Kingdom (c.2686–c.2181 BC). Unfortunately, the wood could not withstand the ravages of time, but the gold work is spectacular. The finials of the carrying poles take the form of elegant palmiform capitals, and the chair is decorated with strips of gold chased in imitation of reed matting. The ebony panels of the backrest are decorated inside and out with exquisite hieroglyphs worked in gold, each one a little masterpiece. The inscription reads:

Mother of the King of Upper and Lower Egypt, follower of Horus, controller of the butchers of the acacia house, one for whom everything she says, is done, the god's bodily daughter, Hetepheres.

There are also two gilded wooden chairs decorated with papyrus clusters and delicate inlay work, as well as a bed and headrest, also of gilded wood. Other objects found in the tomb include a tubular leather case for walking sticks, a large gilded jewellery box containing silver bracelets inlaid with precious stones and a small box containing razors and three elegant golden vessels.

▼ *This narrow side panel from one of the boxes found in Hetepheres' tomb shows the name of her husband, Sneferu.*

▲ *This gilded wooden chair was placed in Hetepheres' tomb for her use in the Afterlife, but was likely to have seen service in her lifetime.*

The body of the queen has not been found. A beautifully carved alabaster sarcophagus was found in the shaft but it was empty. However, an alabaster canopic chest discovered in the tomb was found to contain the queen's internal organs, and it is some of the earliest evidence for the practice of including the organs in the burial in this manner.

However, the American archaeologist Mark Lehner has recently suggested that her original burial place was, in fact, the shaft-grave and it was this that was robbed in antiquity. He thinks her body, but not the canopic chest, was then removed to the satellite pyramid, which was also later violated. This would explain the damage to the funerary

▲ *Furniture found in the tomb of Hetepheres would have been used by her on royal progresses through Egypt, which took place at regular intervals. It included a portable canopy, a chair, a bed and a headrest.*

equipment found in the shaft grave and the presence there of the canopic chest and the empty sarcophagus. ◆

Khufu's Boats

Boat pits as part of a funerary complex are known from the First Dynasty (c.3100–c.2890 BC). Boats have always played a significant role in the lives of the Egyptians, and were also important in a funerary context. In the Pyramid Texts, there are many references to the boat of the sun god Re, and to the fact that the king in his Afterlife expected to accompany Re in his daily journeys across the sky.

Five boat pits are associated with Khufu's burial within the Great Pyramid complex. Two lie to the south of the pyramid, and three others were found to the east. Both of the southern pits were sealed by huge blocks of limestone. One of these was opened and was found to contain a large wooden boat that had been taken apart for storage. This was restored over a period of ten years by Ahmed Yussef Mustafa, and was finally reassembled in 1968. It is now housed in a specially constructed museum nearby. The function of the craft is unknown. It may have been a solar boat, in which the deceased king, identified with the sun god Re, would cross the sky each day. It may have been used as a state barge in real life, or it may have been the boat that brought the king's body from the capital at Memphis to his pyramid for burial. That it might have had a practical use before burial is suggested by the fact that it shows signs of having been in water. Nevertheless, it could also have been part of the funerary equipment intended to provide the king with everything he needed in the next world.

The other pit on the southern side has not yet been opened, although there are plans to do so in the future. However, using modern technology it has been

▶ *One of Khufu's boats reconstructed from timbers found in one of five boat pits surrounding his pyramid is now on display in the Boat Museum at Giza.*

▲ *In this scene from the Valley of the Kings, the sun god Re sails through the Underworld and accompanies the king on his journey to the Afterlife.*

▼ *An aerial view of some of the empty boat pits lying close to the Great Pyramid.*

possible to see inside the pit without opening it. An endoscopic image has been obtained, which proves that there is indeed a boat inside. The other three pits are empty, and it is not known whether they ever contained boats or whether the pits themselves were intended to represent boats.

Khufu's boat was made of cedarwood from Lebanon. Shipments of wood from Byblos are known from the reign of Sneferu (c.2613–c.2589 BC). They are also mentioned on the Fifth Dynasty stela known as the Palermo Stone, which records important events from the beginning of the First Dynasty to the end of the Fifth Dynasty (c.2345). No nails were used in the construction of the boat: the planks were fastened together with ropes and pegs.

The boat is 43m (141ft) long and 6m (20ft) wide. It has a very shallow draught, making it suitable only for use on the River Nile. There are two cabins, a long central one, presumably for the use of the king, and a smaller one at the prow, probably for the captain. Two large steering oars are located in the stern and the boat was rowed by ten pairs of oars. There is no mast and so no provision for a sail. ◆

The Eastern and Western Cemeteries

The Great Pyramid is the central monument in a large necropolis. Behind the three queens' pyramids to the east of Khufu's pyramid, several members of the royal family were buried, some in mastabas and some in rock-cut tombs. The mastabas of the Sixth Dynasty official Qar and his relative Idu are also situated in the Eastern Cemetery. Officials of Khufu's reign lie in mastaba tombs in a cemetery to the west.

The tomb of Meresankh III

One of the most beautiful and best-preserved tombs in the Eastern Cemetery is that of Queen Meresankh III. She was the granddaughter of Khufu and the daughter of two of his children, Kawab and Hetepheres II. She became the wife of her half-brother King Khafre (c.2558– c.2532 BC), and was about 50 years old when she died.

Her tomb lies below that of her mother and consists of a large, subterranean, rock-cut tomb chapel divided into three main sections. The doorway is inscribed with her name and titles, principally 'Daughter of the King' and 'Royal Wife of Khafre'. It also, unusually, records the time taken to mummify her body. The inscription states that 270 days elapsed between the dates of her death and burial, which is an unusually long time. The embalming process and associated ritual is generally thought to have taken about 70 days, so perhaps her tomb was not finished at the time of her death.

In the first section are scenes common to most tombs of the Old Kingdom (c.2686–c.2181 BC). As well as the usual offering scenes, they show farmworkers engaged in agricultural work, fishermen catching fish by various means, hunters in the marshes and fights between the boatmen. Meresankh and Hetepheres are depicted trapping birds in a net and sailing through the marshes in a papyrus boat, gathering lotus flowers.

▼ *Beyond the square pillars of the first large room is an extension containing statues in high relief of Meresankh III, her mother Hetepheres II and several young female members of the family.*

▲ *Meresankh and Hetepheres are depicted gathering lotus and catching birds with nets in the marshes. Both of these activities have religious significance, the lotus being a symbol of new life and the catching of birds representing the restoration of order over chaos.*

Immediately to the left of the entrance are scenes showing scribes, sculptors, goldsmiths and carpenters at work. The section showing the making of statues is particularly interesting because the names of two of the artists are recorded. Most Egyptian art is anonymous, and it is only very rarely that the names of individual artists come to light. One of the five panels shows Rehay painting a statue of Meresankh, while another shows his colleague, the sculptor Inkaf, at work on another statue of the queen.

The groups of actual statues are another unusual feature of this tomb. Further along from the scenes in the sculptors' workshop there are three niches containing six statues in officials' attire. Unfortunately, these are not inscribed, so their names are not known. Almost opposite, in the extension to this first room, is a huge niche with a group of ten large, female statues, who presumably represent Meresankh, her mother and her daughters, although, again, there are no inscriptions to

identify them. The main room also has a false door stela, and offering lists are inscribed on the lintel over the door to the next room. Between the main room and the extension are two pillars decorated in painted, carved relief, with figures of Meresankh wearing a close-fitting dress of white linen. Her two young sons are also shown. One scene shows her father and mother in a papyrus boat.

Beyond the main room is the offerings chapel, decorated with agricultural scenes and others that depict the funerary banquet, where the guests are entertained by singers and musicians. On each side of a false door are two more statue niches. Each houses two statues, presumably of Meresankh and Hetepheres, her mother, placed there to receive offerings.

From the offerings chapel, a shaft leads down to the burial chamber, where George Reisner found a black granite sarcophagus in the course of his excavations in 1927. The mummy of the queen was inside, and this was taken to the Cairo Museum. ▶

▶ *A square pillar in the tomb of Meresankh III shows her dressed in an elegant, close-fitting gown of fine linen. Her two young sons are also depicted. Above her image are her name and titles.*

The mastaba of Qar

Qar lived in the Sixth Dynasty, probably some time during the long reign of Pepi II (c.2278–c.2184 BC). Although he was not an official of Khufu during the king's lifetime, he had responsibilities connected with Khufu's funerary cult and so merited a tomb close to the royal burial place. His titles included 'Overseer of the Pyramid City of Khufu and Menkaure' and 'Supervisor of Priests in the Pyramid of Khafre'. He was also 'Regent of the Pyramid' of Pepi I. His wife, Gefi, was a priestess of Hathor.

Qar's tomb is a stone-built mastaba consisting of a staircase passage, a large main room divided into two sections, and an offering chapel. Like the tomb of Meresankh, it has several interesting sculptures. In a niche in the wall to the left of the entrance is a seated statue of Qar, and on the south wall there is a whole series of statues representing Qar, his young son and other members of his family. The same room has well-preserved scenes showing the presentation of offerings and funeral ritual in painted, carved relief. On the pillar in the centre of this room are Qar's names and titles, together with scenes that show him with his sisters and sitting in a chair with his dog. In the offering chapel, which leads off to the right, is a false door stela.

▼ *Qar's tomb is located near to the pyramids of the kings whose cult he served. This view of the interior shows statues of Qar and his relations carved into the face of the rock.*

▲ *The 6th-Dynasty official Qar and his young son are represented by two statues in his tomb. Qar was in charge of the funerary cult of Khufu, Khafre and Menkaure at Giza.*

The mastaba of Idu

The tomb of Idu, who may be either the father or the son of Qar, is virtually next door. This stone-built mastaba is, in many ways, similar to that of Qar but is much smaller. Idu's tomb has one main room decorated with painted reliefs and rock-cut statues of the deceased and his family. On the jambs of the doorway at the entrance to the tomb are Idu's names and titles, which provide some biographical detail. From these it is clear that he also had duties relating to the funerary cults of the Fourth Dynasty kings. He was inspector of the *wab*-priests of Khufu and Khafre, as well as 'Scribe of the Royal Documents in the Presence of the King'.

The decoration of the tomb is funerary in character. There are few scenes of everyday life, which are otherwise common at this period. The false door stela, where offerings were presented, is in the middle of the east wall and is very unusual in design. A statue of the deceased shows him seated, his hands with upturned palms resting on his knees, as he waits to receive offerings. Above his head is a relief that shows him and his wife seated on each side of an offering table. On the opposite wall are niches containing the statues of Idu and his family. One of the most charming shows Idu wearing his short kilt and official's wig, standing next to his son.

The painted reliefs on the south wall to the left and right of the door are funerary scenes. They show Idu's home, a purification tent and the funeral procession. Facing these, on the back wall, are scenes depicting the preparation of food and drink, dancers and musicians, and the presentation of offerings. Idu oversees these sitting on his palanquin.

The Western Cemetery

Other officials are buried to the west of the Great Pyramid, where there is a whole pyramid 'town' with mastabas laid out in 'streets'. One of the most impressive of these tombs belonged to Iymery, a Fifth Dynasty official who was 'Prophet of Khufu' and 'Overseer of the Great House'. This is a large tomb consisting of an entrance, vestibule, first room, *serdab* (statue room) and offering chapel with a false door stela. Here are the familiar everyday-life scenes that decorate the walls of many of the Old Kingdom tombs. The vestibule has scenes showing carpenters, goldsmiths and sculptors at work. In the first room, there are scenes of cattle-breeding, fishing and fowling in the marshes. The offering chapel has scenes showing offerings being presented to the deceased, who is enjoying the company of his wife and family as musicians and dancers entertain them.

▲ *A detail of a painted relief of Idu before an offering table shows him wearing an official's wig and a wide collar, which he may have received as a reward for his services to the king.*

Although many of these tombs have been known for some time, several others have been discovered recently. One of these belongs to a priest called Kai, who remained in royal service from the reign of Sneferu (c.2613–c.2589 BC) to that of Khafre (c.2558–c.2532 BC). His tomb is decorated with elegant reliefs of the tomb owner and offering scenes, in which the colours look as if they were painted yesterday. ◆

▼ *A painted carved relief from the false door of Idu's tomb shows the deceased and his wife at either side of an offering table.*

False doors

In the offering chapel of a tomb, a stela (stone slab) resembling a door was erected to enable the spirit of the deceased to come out and partake of the daily offerings left in front of it. In some royal tombs, false doors were made of red granite, while in non-royal tombs they were of lime-stone, which was sometimes painted red in imitation of granite.

The Tombs of Pharaoh's Workers

The necropolis containing the tombs of the workers who built the pyramids has only recently come to light. It was found in 1990 when a horse ridden by a tourist stumbled over a low wall, which later turned out to be part of a tomb.

The tombs of this cemetery are very small and inferior in quality to the rather grand stone-built mastabas in the cemeteries of the high officials. They were constructed with odds and ends of different types of building materials left over from the building of pyramids and their associated temples. The first one to be explored was a long vaulted chamber with two false doors. Hieroglyphs in the tomb showed that it belonged to Ptah-shepsesu and his wife. There were three burial shafts at the back of the chamber, so perhaps their son was buried there too. Ptah-shepsesu may have been a supervisor of some sort as his tomb is larger than the others surrounding it. Altogether, about 600 of these small tombs have been found, as well as about 30 larger ones belonging to overseers. The tombs were constructed in all shapes and sizes, many of them appearing to imitate the plans of the tombs of high officials. One has a small ramp, perhaps in imitation of a royal tomb.

Later, an upper part of the necropolis was discovered. Here, the tombs were larger and inscriptions indicated that they were the tombs of the artisans, whereas the lower cemetery seems to have been where the labourers were buried. One of the more imposing tombs was a limestone mastaba with six burial shafts and two false doors carved on its eastern face. Attached to the mastaba was a rock-cut room. The burial was found to be intact, and a sealed niche was found to contain four statues of the deceased, whose name was Intyshedu

▼ *Metalworking processes are common themes in Old Kingdom tombs. Here, the workmen use bellows to increase the heat of the brazier, as depicted in the tomb of Mereruka.*

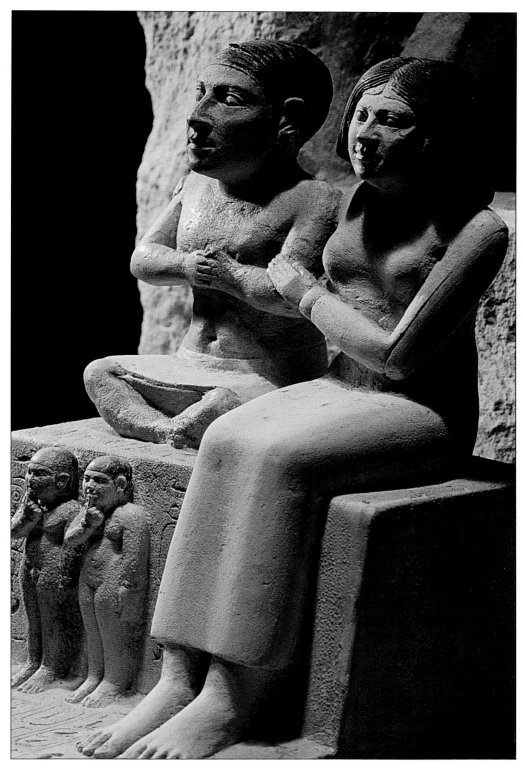

▶ *The dwarf Seneb and his family, from his tomb at Giza (c.2475 BC). Funerary statues project an ideal view of the deceased so Seneb's deformity has been disguised.*

and who styled himself 'Overseer of the Boat of the Goddess, Neith' and 'King's Acquaintance'. He was a carpenter who made ceremonial boats for the goddess Neith on behalf of the king, and the statues depict him at various stages in life, from youth to old age.

None of the workers' bodies had been mummified, and each had been laid in a small shaft in a foetal position. The skeletal remains, especially in the lower cemetery, showed signs of arthritis and joint injuries incurred during lives of hard physical work, and the lifespan of the workers seems to have been shorter than that of the officials and their wives buried in the officials' cemeteries.

The dwarf cemetery

Another important discovery of recent years is that of the dwarf cemetery. Dwarfs were respected members of society in ancient Egypt and often attained high positions at court. The dwarf Seneb, for example, who has been known for many years from his splendid statue in the Cairo Museum, was chief of all the dwarfs who were responsible for the royal wardrobe. He was also a priest involved in the funerary cults of Khufu and Djedefre. It is known from inscriptions on the false door of his tomb that he was a wealthy man who owned cattle. His statue depicts him sitting cross-legged in the position of a scribe, indicating that he was an educated man. Seneb's wife, Senetites, sits beside him with her arm affectionately around his shoulders, in typical Old Kingdom style. The sculptor has sensitively disguised his deformity, ingeniously compensating for his short stature by placing his two children where his legs would otherwise have been.

Among others, a further dwarf tomb was discovered a few years ago. It is of limestone and has two false doors on the east side, where the name of the dwarf, Prnyankhw, is inscribed. Three shafts were discovered, of which one contained his skeletal remains and the others the remains of two women. Statues of these women were found beside the false doors. Prnyankhw's statue is made of black basalt. He is seated on a chair and is shown as a strong and lively man. The only sign of deformity is that his lower left leg appears to be swollen, and it has been suggested that this might indicate the earliest known case of elephantiasis. Like Seneb, Prnyankhw was highly thought of. An inscription on his right leg describes him as 'One who delights his lord every day'. ◆

Memphis and Saqqara

Memphis, about 24km (15 miles) south of Cairo, was the first capital of the united land of Egypt and remained an important religious and administrative centre throughout the Pharaonic Period. It was the chief cult centre of the god Ptah, and in Egyptian mythology it was the place where he performed the act of creation. It was also where the goddesses Isis and Nephthys took the body of their brother Osiris from the Nile, after he had been murdered by his jealous brother Seth, and where Osiris entered the Underworld to become judge of the dead. The divine court, which finally decided that Horus should inherit the throne of Egypt from his father Osiris, was said to have sat at Memphis.

During the Ptolemaic Period (332–30 BC), the new city of Alexandria overtook Memphis in importance. Memphis never recovered its old status, and the ancient buildings were used as a quarry during the building of the new capital, Cairo, after the Arab invasion in the ninth century AD. Today, there is little to see of the ancient capital city. However, the remains of the tombs of kings and commoners at Saqqara, the cemetery site for Memphis, are spectacular.

◀ *Little remains of the ancient city of Memphis, first capital of Egypt and principal cult centre of the creator god Ptah.*

City and Cemetery

According to Herodotus, the city of Memphis was founded by Min, the legendary first king of Egypt, who would appear to be the Menes of the Egyptian kinglists. First, he prepared the site by building a dam to divert the River Nile. He then built the city and embellished it with the 'large and very remarkable temple of Hephaestus' (actually Ptah, the creator god of Memphis, whom the Greeks equated with their own god).

The name of Memphis may be derived from Men-nefer, the name of the pyramid town of Pepi I at Saqqara. It means 'Established and Beautiful'. Other names included 'White Walls', a reference to the city's fortifications, and 'Balance of the Two Lands', referring to its position at the meeting point of the Nile Valley and the Delta.

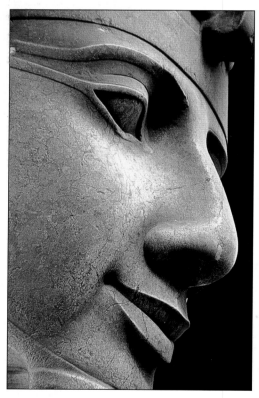

▲ The head of the colossal polished-limestone statue of Ramesses II. Originally erected in front of the Ptah temple, today it is in the museum at Memphis. The statue stood 13m (43ft) high.

Archaeological remains

In Memphis today, a museum housing a gigantic statue of Ramesses II and various other pieces from the New Kingdom (c.1550–c.1069 BC) and later periods are all the tourist usually gets to see of the ancient city. The remains of a Ramesside temple of Ptah are also visible. Material from earlier structures, including a lintel dating from the Middle Kingdom (c.2055–c.1650 BC), was reused in this building, suggesting the existence of previous temples on the site. However, these have not so far come to light as the high water table makes the site difficult to excavate. It is also possible that the city's location changed during the Pharaonic Period, corresponding to changes in the course of the Nile. Recent attempts to locate the most ancient city have been made by David Jeffreys and the Egypt Exploration Society using drill cores.

Close to the temple of Ptah in Memphis was the stall where the Apis bull, the living image of the god Ptah, was kept. On his death, the bull was mummified in the embalming house. The embalming tables used for this purpose remain on the site and the embalming house built by the Twenty-second Dynasty king Sheshonq I (c.945–c.924 BC) is currently undergoing excavation and reconstruction.

Saqqara

Saqqara was the main cemetery site for ancient Memphis, and was used by kings and/or their officials from the First Dynasty (c.3100–c.2890 BC) to the Christian era. Here are the great mastaba tombs of the First Dynasty élite, once thought to be the tombs of the kings of this period. Here, too, is the Step Pyramid of King Djoser (c.2667–c.2648 BC), the oldest stone building in the world. The officials' tombs of the Old Kingdom (c.2686–c.2181 BC) are grouped around the tombs of the kings they served. Most of the Middle Kingdom kings and their officials were buried further south at Dahshur, in the Faiyum, and at Thebes, but because Memphis continued to be the seat of government in the New Kingdom, many officials of this period were buried at Saqqara, although the kings themselves were usually buried in the Valley of the Kings.

Saqqara continued to be used for private burials from the Saite to the Ptolemaic Periods (664–30 BC). After this time the site was abandoned until the fifth century AD, when the Copts (Egyptian Christians) built a monastery here dedicated to St Jeremiah. The tombs of important Persian officials, dating from the Persian occupation of 525–404 BC, are currently being investigated.

The site is vast and extends for about 6km (4 miles) along the desert edge. ◆

▲ A block carved in sunken relief from the pyramid complex of King Unas at Saqqara. The name of the king appears in the cartouches.

Saqqara

N

Tomb of Mereruka

Tomb of Ti

Serapaeum

Tomb of Kagemni

Pyramid of Teti

Pyramid of Userkaf

Step Pyramid of Djoser

Pyramid of Unas

Pyramid Complex of Sekhemkhet

Tombs of Nefer, Niankhkhnum and Khnumhotep, and Neferherenptah

Unas Causeway

The Step Pyramid of King Djoser

The buildings of the Step Pyramid complex of King Djoser (c.2667–c.2648 BC) are of two different types: some were designed for practical use, while the majority are dummy buildings. According to their excavator, Jean-Philippe Lauer, the latter appear to be primarily symbolic and represent the ancient city of Memphis, so that, just as the subterranean chambers of the pyramid were stocked with food and drink to supply the king's supposed physical needs, he was also provided with a capital city for the Afterlife. The functional buildings may have been used during the king's funeral and for the subsequent daily ritual of his mortuary cult.

▼ *The Step Pyramid of King Djoser, built on the desert plateau, is seen here across the date palm trees of the Nile Valley.*

Entrance to the complex

The complex covers a large area in the form of a rectangle 544 x 277m (1,785 x 909ft), 15 hectares (37 acres) in all, which is thought to be the size of a typical large town of the period. Boundary stelae, inscribed with the name of the king and his two daughters, Hetep-her-nebti and Int-ka-s, mark out the site, and it is entirely surrounded by a wall of fine-quality white Tura limestone. This may well have represented the walls of the city, which gave Memphis one of its epithets, 'White Walls'. Fourteen dummy doorways are set in the walls and the complex is entered on the south-eastern side through a doorway with a door carved in an open position. Inside the door is a small vestibule and a corridor composed of two rows of 20 half-engaged fluted columns,

carved in imitation of bundles of reeds. The corridor leads into a small hypostyle hall (a chamber in which the roof is supported by columns) with eight columns arranged in pairs connected by limestone blocks. Beyond is the Great Courtyard in front of the Step Pyramid.

Djoser's pyramid

The Step Pyramid is a tower built in six stages, based on a mastaba 63m (207ft) square and about 8m (26ft) tall. This covers a shaft 28m (92ft) deep, leading to the burial chamber and a whole network of subterranean rooms and tunnels used for funerary goods. A further series of 11 shafts and chambers were constructed to the east, perhaps to accommodate the burial of the royal women. The mastaba seems to have been expanded to cover these extensions, and at some point further stages were added. This produced a more imposing monument and perhaps represented a stairway to heaven, which, according to the Pyramid Texts found in the pyramid of King Unas (c.2375–c.2345 BC), the king expected to climb.

The Great Courtyard

On the south side of the court is a building called the Southern Tomb, which may have housed the king's internal organs (liver, lungs, stomach and intestines), the chamber being too small to take a body. Another theory is that it was intended for the burial of the king's *ka* statue, a representation of his spirit or vital force as his slightly smaller double. The walls are decorated with reliefs showing the king running his *heb sed* race and naming him as Horus Netjerikhet. The top of the tomb wall has a frieze of cobras, which represent the goddess Wadjet, the protector of kings.

The *heb sed*, or royal jubilee festival, usually took place after the king had been on the throne for 30 years and included a re-coronation ceremony, when the king was reinvested in his position and his royal power was renewed. It would seem that provision was made for this to happen in the Afterlife too, so

▲ *This statue of King Djoser was found in the* serdab, *or statue room, of his pyramid. It is now in the Cairo Museum and a replica stands in its place on site.*

that the king could be confirmed in his role eternally. In the centre of the Great Courtyard are a couple of semicircular blocks, two of the markers that once indicated the course to be run by the king during his *sed*-festival in the Afterlife. On the eastern side of the court is Temple T, a building that perhaps represents the pavilion where in real life the king would wait at certain points in the *heb sed* ritual. It contains a niche decorated with *djed*-pillars, which were associated with Osiris and symbolized stability, and the king is likely to have been represented here by a statue. ▶

◀ *Distinctive columns carved to resemble bundles of reeds can be seen when looking east through the colonnaded entrance to Djoser's pyramid complex, which was built by Imhotep.*

◄ A frieze of royal cobras decorates the top of the so-called Southern Tomb.

The *heb sed* court

From Temple T the wall curves round, guiding the ceremonial procession into the *heb sed* court where the king would be recrowned, once as King of Lower Egypt and once as King of Upper Egypt. In this court, there is a platform approached by a short flight of steps. Here, there would have been a double canopy, under which the ceremony would have taken place. A tiny ebony label once attached to grave goods in an Early Dynastic tomb at Abydos depicts this ceremony and enabled archaeologists to reconstruct the platform and short flights of steps. The *heb sed* court is surrounded by dummy chapels with beautifully finished façades of dressed limestone, but entirely filled with rubble. They were designed to provide a suitable setting for the ceremonial. Several unfinished statues of the king have also been found in this area, but their precise intended location is not known.

The Southern and Northern Courts

Leading from the *heb sed* court is the Southern Court, the main feature of

► The heb sed *court in Djoser's Step Pyramid complex was meant to provide a setting for the king's celebration of the* heb sed *in the Afterlife.*

which is the House of the South. Although it is now restored only to doorway height, Jean-Philippe Lauer, the French architect who has restored the complex, thought that the building would originally have been more than 12m (40ft) high, with a façade embellished with slender, engaged fluted columns. Many of the capitals were found, almost complete, lying in the

sand, carved in the form of pendant leaves. Set in a recess in the wall of the court, Lauer found the base of a small round column. He also found the uppermost part of the column, but unfortunately the capital seems to have disappeared. Lauer thought that it would have been in the form of a lotus, the symbol of Southern or Upper Egypt, hence the name given to the court.

Inside the House of the South are some interesting graffiti written by visitors during the New Kingdom (c.1550–c.1069 BC), expressing their admiration for the monument, which was by then about 1,500 years old. One of these is particularly informative because it mentions the name of Djoser, while the other inscriptions in the complex name King Netjerikhet as the owner. It is now recognized that they were one and the same (each king of Egypt having more than one name). This graffito reads:

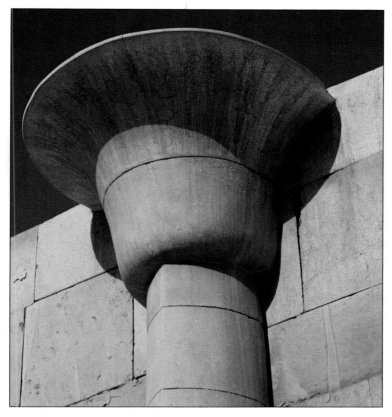

▲ *Papyrus-form pillar with a triangular stem and an open-umbel capital in the so-called Northern Court. The papyrus was the symbol of Lower Egypt.*

The scribe Ahmose, son of Iptah, came to see the temple of Djoser. He found it as though heaven were within it, Re rising in it. Then he said, 'Let loaves and oxen and all good and pure things fall to the ka of the justified Djoser; may heaven drip fresh myrrh, may it drip incense!'

Next comes the Northern Court, the east wall of which has a recess with three slender triangular columns crowned with open papyrus umbels symbolizing Northern or Lower Egypt and emphasizing the dual nature of the complex. Another building, corresponding to the House of the South in the other court, completes this section.

At the north-eastern corner of the pyramid is the *serdab*, or statue chamber, which housed the *ka* statue of the king to which offerings would have

▶ *The entrance to the Step Pyramid complex of King Djoser.*

been brought during the daily mortuary ritual. The original statue is now in the Cairo Museum and has been replaced by a replica. The mortuary temple was on the north side of the pyramid. It is largely in ruins now, but must have been imposing in its time and is the earliest example known. Also on the north side is the original entrance to the burial chamber, although this is no longer accessible to tourists. During the Saite Period (664–525 BC) another entrance was made on the southern side. ◆

Imhotep

The architect of the Step Pyramid of King Djoser was Imhotep, the king's vizier. He has been identified by an inscription on the base of a statue of the king. He was later also credited with medical knowledge, and his fame became so great that in the Ptolemaic Period (332–30 BC) he was deified and equated both with Thoth, the ancient Egyptian god of wisdom, and Asklepios, the ancient Greek god of healing.

The Asklepion, his cult centre, was visited by pilgrims who brought offerings of mummified ibises, many bearing the name of Imhotep on the wrappings. Pilgrims also left clay models of afflicted body parts in the hope that Imhotep would heal them. It was in the search for the actual tomb of Imhotep that the sacred animal cemetery at Saqqara was accidentally found.

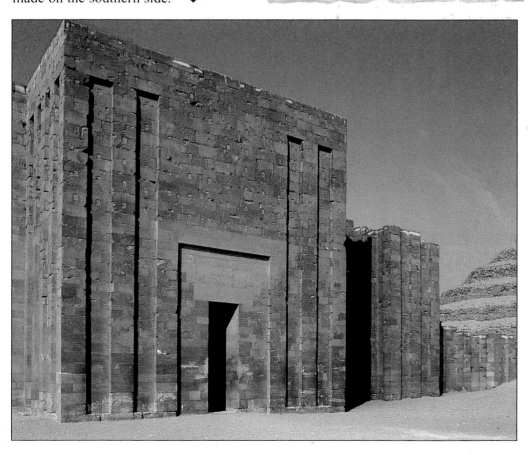

The *Sed*-Festival

The *heb sed*, or royal jubilee festival, was a ritual during which the king's right to rule and his royal powers were renewed. In representations of this ceremony, he is usually shown running alongside the Apis bull, proving his fitness to rule, and then being recrowned as 'King of the Two Lands'. Officially, the *sed-*festival was held after the king had been on the throne for 30 years, but reliefs and inscriptions suggest that some kings, including those with relatively short reigns, celebrated earlier. Although this may sometimes have been the case, other kings may simply have been depicted symbolically fulfilling one of the obligations of kingship, just as Queen Nefertiti, for example, perhaps as co-ruler with her husband, Akhenaten (c.1352–c.1336 BC), is depicted smiting enemies.

The origins of the *sed*-festival are not known, although there is evidence that it was held from the very beginning of recorded history. On a small ebony label once attached to a jar of oil from the tomb of King Den (c.2950 BC) at Abydos, a tiny pin-man figure of the king is shown running around a clearly defined course and carrying the *heb sed* insignia. To the left, there is a platform approached by a short flight of steps, on which a double shrine has been erected. Inside the shrine, the king is shown again, sitting on a throne and wearing the Double Crown, having been recrowned twice, once as King of Upper Egypt and once as King of Lower Egypt.

The *heb sed* and the Afterlife

The Step Pyramid complex of King Djoser at Saqqara includes provision for this ceremony to be eternally re-enacted

▶ *Queen Hatshepsut in her role as king of Egypt celebrates the* heb sed *by symbolically running around Egypt's boundaries accompanied by the Apis bull.*

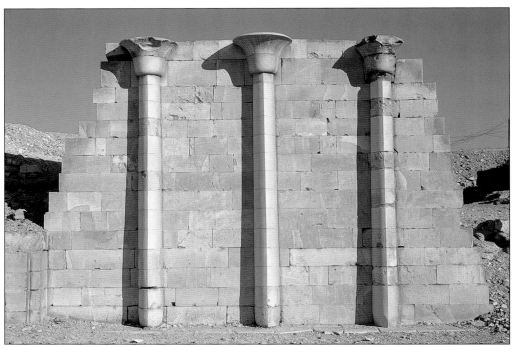

in his Afterlife. The markers in the Great Court that indicated the course the king would have to run perhaps represented the frontiers of Egypt and symbolized the extent of the king's dominion. The figure of the running king can be seen in low relief in the chambers below the Southern Tomb and beneath the pyramid.

▲ *Papyrus-form columns embellish the walls of the House of the North in the Step Pyramid complex, papyrus being the symbol of Lower Egypt.*

Evidence for the view that the king would expect to take part in this important ritual of kingship in the Afterlife is found in a beautiful alabaster vase that was discovered in one of the chambers beneath the pyramid itself. The vase is carved with the figure of a man with arms upraised, holding aloft a square object, perhaps a canopy, although Jean-Philippe Lauer suggests that it is the platform on which the double shrine and the two thrones would have been set up. The handle of the vase is decorated with reliefs of the thrones of the Two Lands. The figure represents the hieroglyph for millions of years and the thrones are those used by the king at his *heb sed*.

The *heb sed* in history

The ritual was practised throughout Pharaonic history. At Karnak, blocks from the reconstructed Red Chapel of Hatshepsut (c.1473–c.1458 BC) show her, as king, running with the Apis bull between the markers. Scenes from the inner walls of the hypostyle hall in the temple at Karnak show Ramesses II (c.1279–c.1213 BC) similarly engaged. Jubilees are also depicted in the mortuary temple of Amenhotep III (c.1390–c.1352 BC) at Thebes, although he seems to have altered the ritual and

▶ *King Djoser, dressed in his* heb sed *costume, runs around the course markers that symbolized the boundaries of Egypt.*

its usual setting somewhat. He celebrated three *heb seds* and descriptions of the ceremonies say that they took place on the great artificial lake he had created at Malkata. Here, the king and statues of the deities sailed along in barges, re-enacting the voyage of the sun god through the Underworld.

Surprisingly, in view of the break with tradition during the reign of the Eighteenth Dynasty king Akhenaten, the *heb sed* was also depicted in the colonnaded court of the Temple of Aten at Karnak, although in this case Akhenaten's queen, Nefertiti, and the royal daughters also took part. The ceremony also took place very early in his reign, before the move to the new capital of Akhetaten. Another remarkable feature is that the Aten, the life-giving disc of the sun, is also seen taking part in a *heb sed* of his own. This is most unusual because the gods are usually seen to give *sed*-festivals to the king; they are never shown taking part in such a ritual themselves. Akhenaten seems to be pointing out that because the god is king, so the king is also a god.

The festival continued to take place in later times. This is confirmed by scenes from the temple of the cat-goddess, Bastet, at Bubastis, where the Twenty-second Dynasty king Osorkon II (c.874–c.850 BC) is shown seated in the *heb sed* kiosk, wearing the typical robe. At Kom Ombo, carved reliefs show Ptolemy VIII (170–116 BC) receiving *heb sed* symbols from the god Horus, showing that even foreign kings liked to depict themselves taking part in the traditional ritual of kingship. ◆

◀ *The* heb sed *court in the Step Pyramid complex makes provision for the king to renew his right to rule in the Afterlife for all eternity.*

The Pyramid of King Unas

The pyramid of King Unas (c.2375–c.2345 BC), the last king of the Fifth Dynasty, is located near the south-western corner of the Step Pyramid complex. Most of the outer casing has disappeared from this pyramid, revealing its inner core of loose blocks and rubble. It is the smallest of all the Old Kingdom pyramids, but also one of the most interesting as it has several unusual features. On the south side of the pyramid, for instance, there is an inscription of Khaemwese, son of the Nineteenth Dynasty king Ramesses II (c.1279–c.1213 BC), saying that he restored the pyramid on his father's instructions and replaced the name of King Unas because by that time it was missing.

The entrance is on the north side of the pyramid at ground level, and was originally closed with a limestone plug. A sloping passage only 1.4m (4ft 6in) high leads to a vestibule and a second corridor, where there are the remains of three granite portcullises. This corridor eventually leads to a small rectangular room with three niches, probably

▼ *Although Unas' pyramid was repaired in antiquity, the outer casing has almost disappeared.*

intended for the *ka* statues of the king. A passage leads to the burial chamber, in which Gaston Maspero of the Egyptian Antiquities Service found a basalt sarcophagus containing the remains of a mummy in 1881.

Pyramid Texts

Both the rectangular antechamber and the burial chamber have ceilings made of two large, sloping limestone slabs decorated with gold stars on a blue ground. The walls of both chambers are covered with Pyramid Texts, and this is

▲ *A roofed causeway ran from the valley temple to the mortuary temple. Next to it were two large boat pits.*

the earliest known appearance of these collections of spells, which were intended to enable the king to overcome hostile forces and powers in the Underworld, and so to join the sun god Re, his divine father. He would then spend his days in eternity, sailing with Re across the sky in the solar boat:

Re-Atum, this Unas comes to you,
A spirit indestructible...
Your son comes to you, this Unas
*   comes to you,*
May you cross the sky united in
*   the dark,*
May you rise in lightland, the place
*   in which you shine!*
(Utterance 217)

The sky's reed floats are launched
*   for Re,*
That he may cross on them to
*   lightland...*
The sky's reed floats are launched
*   for Unas,*
That he may cross on them to
*   lightland, to Re...*
(Utterance 263)

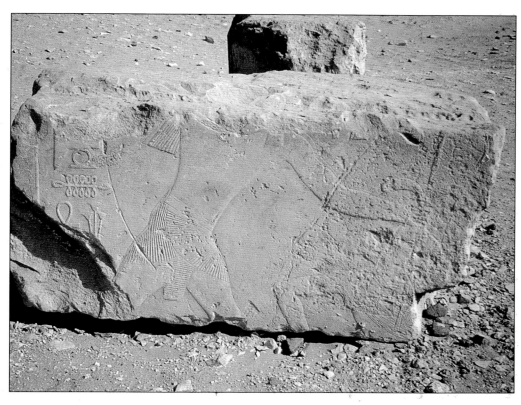

Other spells describe the king climbing a ladder to heaven and joining the gods among the stars, or acting as Re's secretary:

Unas squats before him,
Unas opens his boxes,
Unas unseals his decrees,
Unas seals his dispatches,
Unas sends his messengers who
  tire not,
Unas does what Unas is told.
(Utterance 309)

The hieroglyphs of the texts are beautifully carved and filled with blue paste, so that they stand out boldly from the white background. Several kings of the Sixth Dynasty, Teti (c.2345–c.2323 BC), Pepi I (c.2321–c.2287 BC), Merenre (c.2287–c.2278 BC) and Pepi II (c.2278– c.2184 BC), also decorated their burial chambers in this way.

The pyramid complex

The mortuary temple of Unas was partly excavated by the Italian archaeologist Alessandro Barsanti in the early twentieth century, and more completely by Sir Charles Firth in 1929. It is almost completely destroyed, although it has been possible to trace the layout. The temple was similar to that of Sahure, although the floor was made of alabaster rather than basalt.

The plan of the temple is not known in its entirety as the remains of the building lie partly under a modern road. However, enough work has been done to show that the temple was embellished with beautifully made granite palmiform columns. There was a lake here, which made a harbour for the temple. The archaeologists also

▲ *The causeway was decorated with scenes in carved and painted relief. Here, Unas is depicted smiting his enemies.*

discovered the harbour, including quays and a slipway.

Linking the valley and mortuary temples is an impressive causeway, 750m (2,460ft) long and decorated with once brightly coloured reliefs. The scenes are amazingly varied. Some show agricultural work, others hunters pursuing lions, leopards, hyenas and a giraffe. Ships are depicted transporting granite palmiform columns, and craftsmen work copper and gold. Possibly the most intriguing are the famine scenes. The relief is not complete and it is not possible to identify the starving people with any certainty. Amelia Edwards surmised that they were foreigners to whom Unas probably sent aid, and that the scenes illustrated one of his good deeds that he wished to perpetuate for eternity. Others see them as Egyptian and read into the scenes signs of Egypt's decline towards the end of the Old Kingdom. ◆

◀ *The walls of the long, roofed causeway were also elaborately decorated with beautifully carved hieroglyphs.*

Tombs of Old Kingdom Officials

Alongside the causeway linking the mortuary and valley temples of King Unas (c.2375–c.2345 BC), there are several tombs belonging to officials of the Old Kingdom (c.2686–c.2181 BC). They chose to be buried near to the pyramids of their royal masters so that they could be on hand to continue to serve them in the Afterlife.

The tomb of Nefer

One of the best-preserved is that of Nefer, but it can be visited only with special permission. Nefer was 'Head of the Royal Singers' and 'Inspector of the Court'. He seems to have been close to the king because he calls himself 'keeper of the king's secrets'. Several members of his family were buried here, including his father, Kaha, who also held the position of 'Head of the Royal Singers', and his mother, Khons, who was a priestess of the goddess Hathor. In the tomb, Nefer's father is described as the 'controller of the beautiful voice' and 'unique among the singers of the funerary estate'. Nefer's three sons and his daughter were also musical and had positions as professional singers. The family is depicted in the tomb, which is noteworthy for a unique scene in which Nefer's wife and child are shown watching dancers.

The tomb is very beautifully decorated with lively scenes in painted relief. Some show work going on in a vegetable garden, where onions and lettuce are being planted and grapes are being gathered and pressed. A baboon is lending a hand. Papyrus is being gathered and prepared for transportation, cattle mate and calves are born. An interesting group shows the building of a wooden cargo boat, the construction of a canoe and a papyrus boat. Elsewhere,

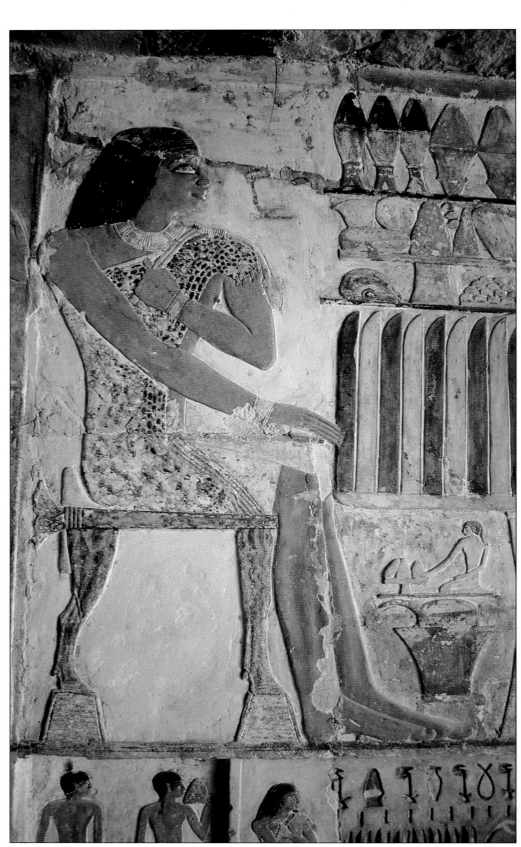

▶ *Nefer, dressed in the leopardskin of a priest, sits in front of an offering table laden with loaves of bread. Above are jars of wine, beer and fruit.*

▶ *Papyrus plants are harvested and bound into bundles in preparation for transport. Papyrus was used for paper, making sandals and building boats.*

ships ply up and down the Nile. As usual, much attention is paid to hunting, fishing and the preparation of food.

A pit cut into the floor of the tomb houses one of the oldest mummies extant. It is about 4,500 years old and, even though the mummification process had not been perfected at this stage, it is virtually intact. It had been so carefully wrapped that the bandages bore the impressions of the fingernails and a callus on the sole of the foot. The body was naked apart from a bead collar. A false beard had also been added. When the body was discovered in the 1940s, the deceased was holding his long official's cane in one hand and a short staff in the other. It is not certain whether it is Nefer himself who is lying here, or a family friend called Waty.   ▶

The king's officials

The Narmer Palette, which dates from the beginning of the Dynastic Period, and labels attached to grave goods found at Abydos and Saqqara give the names of officials who held positions in the administration of Egypt. These make it clear that an organized central administration existed from the very beginning of the united land, c.3100 BC. Officials carried titles such as 'Sandal Bearer', 'Sole Companion' or 'Royal Seal Bearer'. The 'Chief of Scouts' organized trading expeditions to procure exotic goods for the king.

▶ *Nefer's tomb is one of the most beautifully decorated of the Old Kingdom. Here, a servant brings a deer to sustain Nefer in the Afterlife.*

also a fine fowling scene with a large flock of birds, from which the tomb gets its nickname.

The mastaba of Mereruka

Mereruka held office as vizier during the reign of Teti (c.2345–c.2323 BC), the first king of the Sixth Dynasty, and married the king's daughter. His tomb lies close to Teti's pyramid. It was excavated by Jacques de Morgan of the Egyptian Antiquities Service in 1892, and it is the largest of all the non-royal Old Kingdom tombs. There are 32 chambers in all: 17 are in the main suite, which accommodated the funerary arrangements of Mereruka himself, and the rest were used for the burials of his wife, Watetkhethor, and their son, Meryteti. Most of the rooms are decorated, and those that are not were used for stores.

The tomb of Niankhkhnum and Khnumhotep

Niankhkhnum and Khnumhotep were brothers, probably twins. Like Nefer, they were high-ranking officials. Each held the position of 'Prophet of Re' in the sun temple of Niuserre (c.2445– c.2421 BC) and both were 'Overseers of the Manicurists of the Great House'. They are beautifully depicted, embracing each other, on the wall of the chamber leading to the offering room.

The superstructure of their tomb was almost completely destroyed in antiquity, because King Unas built his causeway over it. It has been reconstructed using the decorated blocks that were found during excavation, and is now open to the public. The part of the tomb that was cut into the rock is well preserved. The quality of the painted reliefs is excellent, especially in the first of the rock-cut chambers. The various scenes on the western side of the tomb include fishing and fowling in the marshes, stock breeding, papyrus gathering and fights among the boatmen. Opposite are agricultural scenes and scenes of sculptors and jewellers at work. There are also the usual offering bearers and banqueting scenes, where the guests are entertained with music and dancing.

The 'bird tomb' of Neferherenptah

Nearer to the boat pit of the pyramid complex of Unas is the mastaba of Neferherenptah, who was 'Head of the Hairdressers'. This tomb is unfinished, and it would appear that building was interrupted by the construction of the causeway of King Unas. However, it is decorated with simple designs of exceptionally high quality. The scenes depict agricultural work and the preparation of food and drink. There is

▼ Kagemni's tomb is decorated with scenes showing many types of fishing. Here, fish are being caught in baskets and nets from a papyrus boat.

▶ *Lively scenes showing fights between boatmen in the marshes are common in later Old Kingdom tombs. This one comes from the tomb of Kagemni.*

Mereruka appears on the entrance to the tomb together with his name and titles. Just inside the vestibule he is shown hunting in the papyrus marshes, where birds, hippopotamuses and crocodiles are vividly portrayed. In the next room, Mereruka and his wife inspect a jeweller's workshop. All the processes are recorded, from the weighing out of the gold to the making up of the finished pieces. Several of the workers are dwarfs. Other scenes show sculptors, carpenters and makers of stone vases at work.

The main room, the funerary chapel, has a false door in which stands a life-sized painted statue of Mereruka, who appears to be striding forward to receive his offerings of food and drink. The roof is supported by six square pillars, and Mereruka appears on each face carrying his staffs of office. The walls are decorated with a variety of scenes in painted relief. To the right of the statue,

▼ *A detail of a beautifully carved relief from the tomb of Kagemni, showing cattle crossing a stream.*

another figure of Mereruka watches boys and girls playing boisterous games, while to the left there are some unusual scenes where animals, including hyenas, are being force-fed. Nearer to the entrance agricultural work is being carried out on Mereruka's estates, and on the opposite wall several large ships get ready to sail.

Although in poor condition, this tomb has some charming domestic scenes. The walls of Chamber 7 show Mereruka and his wife sitting together on a large couch, while she plays her harp to soothe him. Just to the left they are shown again, this time standing hand in hand while servants make their bed. On the opposite wall they receive offerings and are entertained by male and female dancers.

In the area devoted to Mereruka's wife, she is shown being carried on a large sedan chair and receiving offerings in the company of her son and daughter. In another scene, she is portrayed with her three dogs and a pet monkey.

The mastaba of Kagemni

Kagemni was vizier, or chief minister, in the early part of Teti's reign. His large tomb also lies opposite Teti's pyramid, next door to that of Mereruka. Eight of its rooms are beautifully decorated in high relief. There are also five storage areas. The tomb has some unusual features. One is that the *serdab*, or statue chamber, which housed the *ka* statue, is completely sealed off from the rest of the tomb. (There is usually a 'window' from which the statue can see out.) There is also a stairway leading to the roof and two boat-shaped chambers reminiscent of the boat pits of King Unas.

Much of the decoration in Kagemni's tomb is taken up with offering processions, agricultural work and stock breeding. Some of the best scenes are of fishing, and show several different methods of catching fish, including the use of clap nets, trawl nets and a multi-hooked rod. Other scenes show birds trapped in a net and hippopotamuses speared with harpoons. Unusual themes include a piglet being fed and a mother feeding her baby on a boat. Kagemni himself is seen receiving offerings. ◆

New Kingdom Tombs at Saqqara

Saqqara continued to be used as a necropolis in the New Kingdom (c.1550–c.1069 BC). The necropolis was known in the mid-nineteenth century from the work of Carl Lepsius and from loose sculpted and inscribed blocks that had found their way into museums, but some of the most important discoveries of recent times have been made by the joint expedition of the Egypt Exploration Society and Leiden University, headed by Professor Geoffrey Martin.

The tomb of Maya

One of the tombs seen by Lepsius was that of Maya, treasurer of Tutankhamun (c.1336–c.1327 BC) and his two immediate successors in the Eighteenth Dynasty. Maya's tomb was found almost by accident when the EES–Leiden team were led astray by the inaccuracies in Lepsius' map of the necropolis. In 1986, while they were excavating in the tomb of Ramose, a contemporary of Maya and an officer in the Egyptian army, they noticed a shaft leading to the underground chambers of another tomb. Much to their delight it turned out to be the tomb of Maya, which they had been seeking and had so far failed to locate. The following year they began to explore the superstructure and soon found the tops of the mudbrick walls of the inner court and the main cult room with its adjoining chapels. These areas were cleared of sand and the reliefs revealed.

The tomb is decorated with painted, carved reliefs of the highest quality, and with texts that identify the owner and his wife, Meryt. Some that Lepsius had recorded were no longer there. These included some that he had taken to Berlin, but others seem to have been removed by local people and used to make lime. This also seems to have been the fate of several statues known to have been made for the tomb, although three, which were in perfect condition and are

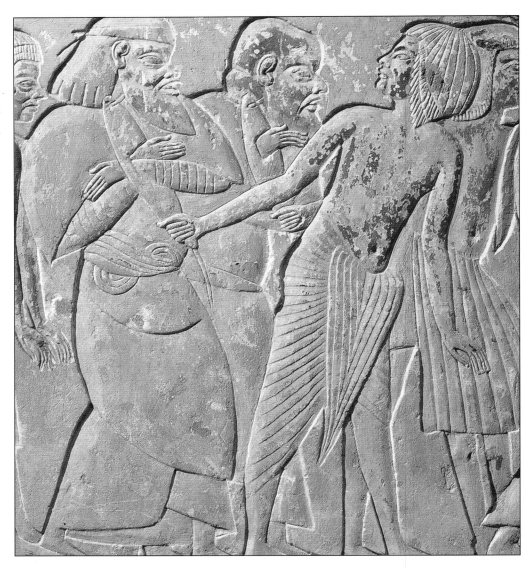

▲ Prisoners from the city-states of Syria–Palestine are led by Egyptian soldiers into the presence of Tutankhamun.

masterpieces of Egyptian art, had been acquired by the Leiden Museum in the 1820s and have thus survived. However, the statue group of Maya and Meryt, which Lepsius had noticed, was still there, albeit lying face downwards instead of standing upright against the wall. This revealed the fact that it had been made from a block taken from an Old Kingdom tomb. In fact, much of the material used in the building of this tomb had been 'recycled' in this way.

Some detail concerning the life of Maya was found in an inscription on the south wall of the entrance pylon, or gateway. He wrote about himself thus:

...the governance which came into being through me, [was] as something ordained by my god since my youth, the presence of the king having been granted to me since I was a child. I happily reached the end [of my career], enjoying countless favours of the Lord of the Two Lands...In the beginning I was good, in the end I was excellent, one who was revered in peace in the temple of Ptah. I carried out the

plans of the king of my time without neglecting anything he had commanded...[I made splendid] the temples, fashioning the images of the gods for whom I was responsible. I entered face to face to the August Image...

The tomb of Horemheb

Maya's great contemporary was the army commander Horemheb, who later became the last king of the Eighteenth Dynasty (c.1323–c.1295 BC) and was buried in the Valley of the Kings. In the earlier part of his career, he prepared a tomb at Saqqara. This tomb was also found by happy accident in 1975, when the joint EES–Leiden expedition was given permission by the Egyptian Antiquities Department to search for the tomb of Maya. Strangely enough, only a few days after starting work, the team came upon a column that bore the image, name and titles of Horemheb, who was already well known to scholars through inscriptions and reliefs in most of the major museums.

Horemheb's tomb is approached by an undecorated pylon, or gateway, leading to the first court. This is mainly decorated with scenes from his time in office and

▼ *Horemheb receives envoys from Libya and the Near East on behalf of Tutankhamun.*

processions of offering bearers. One is a 'Window of Appearances' scene, which shows Horemheb being rewarded by the king for his services. On the west wall of this court there was originally a stela depicting Horemheb worshipping Re-Horakhty, the sun god, Thoth, the god of wisdom, and Maat, the goddess of truth. It was also inscribed with a long hymn in their honour. The original is in the British Museum in London, but a cast now replaces it on the site.

From inscriptions in his tomb, a great deal is known about Horemheb's career. He had a great many titles conferred on him, many by Tutankhamun, although his military career probably began under Akhenaten (c.1352–c.1336 BC). Among these titles are 'Hereditary Prince and Count', 'Deputy of the King in the Entire Land', 'Overseer of all Offices of the King', 'Generalissimo', 'King's Envoy',

▲ *Nubian prisoners of war are very realistically portrayed awaiting transportation to a work camp.*

'Overseer of Recruits of the King of the Two Lands', 'Chief of the Entire Land', 'Sealbearer of the King of Upper and Lower Egypt', 'Overseer of all Overseers of Scribes of the King', 'Overseer of all Works of the King in Every Place' and 'Overseer of All Divine Offices'. It was extremely important that all this was recorded so that Horemheb would be able to continue to serve the king in these capacities in the Afterlife. It was his wife Mutnodjmet, possibly the sister of Akhenaten's wife Nefertiti, who was buried here, while Horemheb enjoyed a royal burial at Thebes. ◆

▼ *Carved in delicate low relief, Maya adores Osiris. The hand of his wife, Meryt, also raised in adoration, is shown behind him.*

The Serapaeum

The Serapaeum was used for the burials and funerary cult of the Apis bulls, which were regarded as the living representation of the Memphite creator god Ptah during their lifetime and were identified with Osiris after death. Herodotus describes the birth and appearance of the Apis bull in Book Three of *The Histories*:

This Apis is the calf of a cow which is never afterwards able to have another. The Egyptian belief is that a flash of light descends upon the cow from heaven, and this causes her to receive Apis. The Apis-calf has distinctive marks: it is black, with a white diamond on its forehead, the image of an eagle on its back, the hairs of its tail double and a scarab under its tongue.

The bulls lived for about 15 years, and when one died its body was taken to be mummified in the special embalming house at Memphis. It then went to the underground galleries of the Serapaeum for burial in a huge granite sarcophagus.

The Serapaeum was first discovered by Richard Pococke in 1738, and then rediscovered and excavated by Auguste Mariette in 1851. Mariette said that he had been led to the Serapaeum and the associated temple by a passage in the work of the Greek geographer and historian, Strabo, who described the avenue of sphinxes leading to it as being virtually buried by drifting sand, 'some having only their heads above the surface'. One day, as Mariette was walking in the desert, he came across the head of a sphinx just visible above the sand, and was immediately reminded of the passage in Strabo. He excavated the site, and found a vast complex of galleries that date from at least the early New Kingdom (c.1550 BC) and which were expanded in the Saite and Ptolemaic Periods.

The catacombs

The galleries were extended during the time of Ramesses II (c.1279-c.1213 BC) and his son Khaemwese, who was High Priest of Ptah at Memphis. Another extension took place in the Saite Twenty-sixth Dynasty (664–525 BC) and they continued in use until the Ptolemaic Period (332–30 BC), when a further gallery was added. The galleries were cut into the solid rock and the burial chambers hewn out on both sides. These chambers house the enormous sarcophagi, which weigh up to 80 tons and measure about 4m (13ft) in length by 2m (6ft 6in) in width, with a height of 3.3m (11ft).

Altogether, 24 sarcophagi were discovered by Mariette, and all but one had been robbed. It seems this tomb had defeated the robbers because the lid was so firmly fixed that Mariette had to resort to dynamite to blast it off.

▲ *The Apis bull, who represented the creator god Ptah while alive and Osiris after death, was kept in a stall outside the Temple of Ptah at Memphis.*

▼ *Large numbers of bronze statuettes of Apis have been found, indicating the popularity of the cult in the Late and Ptolemaic Periods.*

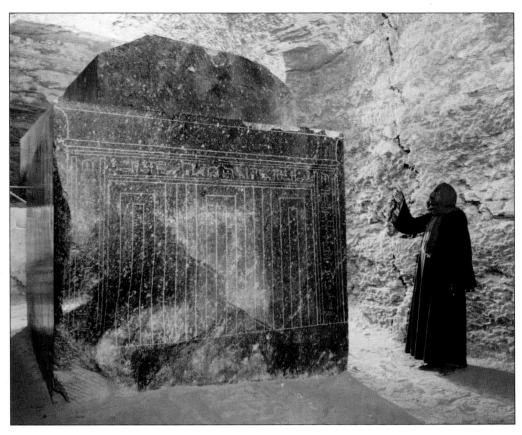

▲ *After death, the Apis bulls were mummified and placed in huge granite sarcophagi weighing up to 80 tons each.*

Inside he found the solid gold statue of a bull, now in the Louvre, Paris, and the mummy of the bull itself, which is now in the Agricultural Museum in Cairo. Elsewhere in the catacombs, Mariette thought that he had found the remains of the mummy of Khaemwese, although some scholars now think that the bones were actually those of a bull.

Mariette was obviously moved by his discoveries:

By some inexplicable accident one of the chambers of the Apis tombs, walled up in the thirtieth year of Ramesses II, had escaped the general plunder of the monuments, and I was so fortunate to find it untouched. Three thousand seven hundred years had had no effect in altering its primitive state. The fingermark of the Egyptian who set the last stone in the wall built to cover up the door was still visible in the mortar. Bare feet had left their traces on the sand...

Votive tablets

What the robbers either overlooked or thought to be worthless were the 500 votive tablets dedicated in antiquity by pilgrims to the site. These, too, are now in the Louvre and, because they are

dated, have proved invaluable for establishing the chronology of the Saite and Graeco-Roman Periods. Their use was demonstrated over a century ago. According to Herodotus, Cambyses (525–522 BC), one of the Persian rulers of Egypt, stabbed the Apis bull in a fit of jealous rage, after which 'Apis lay some time pining in the temple, but at last died of his wound and the priests buried him secretly'. Amelia Edwards, however, noted that one of the votive tablets stated that the bull did not die until the fourth year of the reign of Darius I (522–486 BC), the succeeding king. Herodotus may simply have used this tale to confirm his belief that Cambyses was mad, as this would have been considered such a heinous crime. ◆

▼ *Niches in the walls of the Serapaeum originally contained votive tablets set up by pilgrims to the vaults. These were taken by Mariette to the Louvre and are an invaluable source of information on chronology.*

The Valley of the Kings

From the beginning of the New Kingdom (c.1550–c.1069 BC), kings were no longer buried in pyramids in the north of Egypt but in tombs cut into the cliffs of the Valley of the Kings on the west bank of the Nile at Thebes. Throughout the New Kingdom, Thebes was an important religious and administrative centre. The kings were often in residence there, and the Valley of the Kings became the obvious location for their last resting place. During this period, the king was himself regarded as a god. The walls of royal tombs are covered with scenes depicting the pharaoh in the company of the gods on his journey through the Underworld and finally united with them in paradise. It was therefore natural that the Valley of the Kings should have been regarded as one of the most sacred sites of the Two Lands.

For the ancient Egyptians, death was not the end but the entrance to eternal life. Those who could afford to spent the greater part of their adult lives making preparations for it. Soon after his coronation, the king would instigate work on his tomb, where his transfiguration, resurrection and final union with the gods would take place. A suitable spot would be chosen, a plan drawn up, and the decoration of the walls decided.

◀ *From the beginning of the New Kingdom, royalty were buried in the remote Valley of the Kings on the west bank of the Nile.*

The Royal Burial Ground

The Valley of the Kings must have been wild and remote in ancient times. It is still possible to get the feel of the place by approaching the Valley along the mountain path from Deir el-Medina, as the craftsmen did 3,500 years ago on their way to work on the royal tombs. Even today, when motor coaches follow each other nose to tail along the approach roads and disgorge their passengers at the new rest-house, a sense of eternity pervades the site, defying the attempts of the little tourist trains plying their trade along the Valley to bring it into the twenty-first century.

The Valley of the Kings is actually two valleys. Most of the royal tombs are situated in the eastern valley, with the exception of those of Amenhotep III (c.1390–c.1352 BC) and Ay (c.1327–c.1323 BC), which are in the more remote western branch. The area seems to have been chosen because of its situation, remote from the city of Thebes and the village settlements down by the Nile, perhaps in the hope that the royal

burials would be safe from the activities of the tomb robbers. If so, this proved to be a rather vain hope. When the tombs were excavated in the nineteenth and twentieth centuries, all were found to have been robbed except for that of

▲ From the beginning of the New Kingdom, the kings were no longer buried in pyramids but in rock-cut tombs in the remote Valley of the Kings.

Tutankhamun. That, too, had been entered, but was saved by the necropolis priests.

However, there seems to have been another, perhaps more cogent reason for the location of the royal tombs. From a distance, the mountains of the west bank resemble the hieroglyph *akhet* (horizon). Since the sun set in the west, the ancient Egyptians associated it with the entry of the deceased into the Underworld. The *akhet* hieroglyph of the Theban massif, therefore, became the horizon below which the king entered the Underworld, just as the sun god, in the form of the setting sun, did each night. This belief was acted out each time a royal funeral procession wound its way over the mountain from the mortuary temple and down into the Valley of the Kings, sinking like the sun beyond the western horizon. ◆

◀ Tutankhamun and his wife Ankhesenamun are seen here in an intimate scene from the gilded wooden statue shrine discovered in his tomb.

The Valley of the Kings

① KV1 Ramesses VII
② KV2 Ramesses IV
③ KV5 Sons of Ramesses II
④ KV6 Ramesses IX
⑤ KV7 Ramesses II
⑥ KV8 Merenptah
⑦ KV9 Ramesses V/VI
⑧ KV14 Tawosret and Sethnakhte
⑨ KV15 Seti II
⑩ KV16 Ramesses I
⑪ KV17 Seti I
⑫ KV20 Hatshepsut
⑬ KV34 Tuthmosis III
⑭ KV35 Amenhotep II
⑮ KV38 Tuthmosis I
⑯ KV43 Tuthmosis IV
⑰ KV46 Yuya and Tuya
⑱ KV47 Siptah
⑲ KV57 Horemheb
⑳ KV62 Tutankhamun

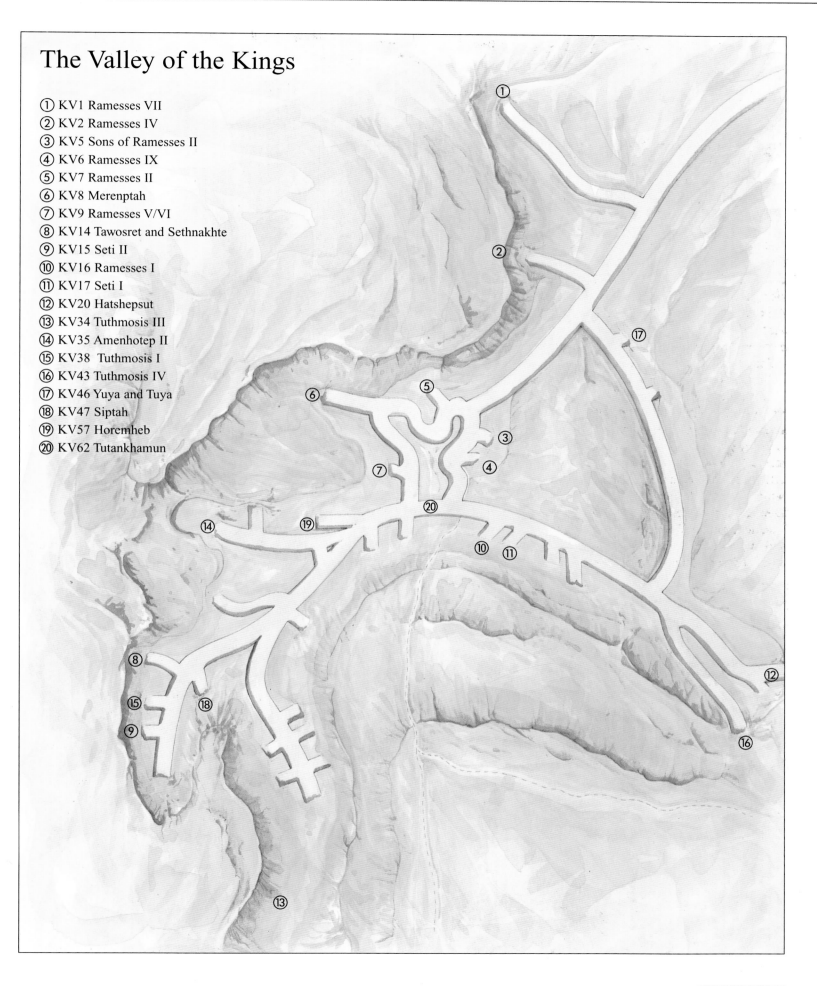

The Burial of the King

The tombs in the Valley of the Kings are radically different from those of the Pyramid Age. During the New Kingdom (c.1550–c.1069 BC) the royal tombs were not built of stone or mudbrick but were laboriously cut into the mountainside. Whereas the interior chambers of the pyramids had been relatively small and mainly undecorated, the passages and burial chambers of the rock-cut tombs were much larger and were brilliantly decorated with images of the king before the gods and with new texts that would ensure his safe arrival in the Afterlife and his union with both Re and Osiris.

Another distinguishing feature is that the mortuary temple, causeway and valley temple were physically separated from the tomb, although spiritually still connected. The temples now lay on the other side of the mountain, on the desert edge of the Nile Valley. The mortuary temples were grander than the earlier ones, while the valley temples were reduced to little more than landing stages, where the boats of the royal funeral procession would dock. The stone-built causeway was replaced in the later New Kingdom by a canal that led to a small harbour in front of the mortuary temple.

Concealed entrances

The location of the tomb and the basic plan, as well as the images and texts chosen for the decoration, varied from period to period. In the earlier part of the Eighteenth Dynasty (c.1550–c.1295 BC), the royal tombs were usually cut higher up the cliffs of the Valley than those of the later kings, and were often near a cleft in the rock. After the burial had taken place, these tombs were blocked with stones and plastered over. Debris deposited by rainwater pouring down the cleft would then conceal the entrance. Because the tombs of the later Eighteenth and Nineteenth Dynasties (c.1550–c.1186 BC) were built lower

▼ *A scene from the tomb of Ramesses I depicts the king flanked by the falcon-headed 'soul of Pe' and the jackal-headed 'soul of Nekhen' representing Upper and Lower Egypt respectively.*

down the valley, they have been subjected to damage by floodwater.

The latest group of tombs, those of the Twentieth Dynasty (c.1186–c.1069 BC), show no sign of any attempt having been made to seal or hide the entrance. These tombs were simply closed with wooden doors. They were often located at ground level at the ends of rocky spurs, and were protected to some extent by the water channels that ran down each side, although some have suffered from water seeping in through cracks in the rock or from storm damage.

Tomb layouts

The plans of the tombs, although basically consisting in each case of a series of descending corridors, an antechamber and a burial chamber, also varied. The typical tomb plan of the earlier Eighteenth Dynasty was perhaps derived from the general layout used in the pyramids of the Old Kingdom

(c.2686–c.2181 BC), and follows a 'bent' axis: a flight of steps leads to three corridors, each known as one of the passages of the sun's nightly journey through the Underworld. This theme is later echoed in the decoration of the walls. Next comes a well or pit, which was perhaps intended to inhibit the activities of tomb robbers, or perhaps simply to drain off water and prevent

▲ The sarcophagus of Tuthmosis IV is decorated with images of the funerary deities, who protect the royal body, and with magical spells, which ensure the king's safe arrival in the Afterlife.

damage to the tomb. Beyond the well is a small pillared hall. Then the tomb takes a right-angled turn, and a further flight of steps and a sloping ramp lead down into the burial chamber.

Over time, the plans became more complicated. More rooms and passages were added, and it could be that these echo the twists and turns seen in maps of the Underworld, which decorate the floors of the rectangular wooden coffins of officials during the Middle Kingdom (c.2055–c.1650 BC).

From the time of Horemheb (c.1323–c.1295 BC), the last king of the Eighteenth Dynasty, the bent-axis plan was abandoned in favour of the 'jogged-axis' or straight type. Although the passages leading to Horemheb's own burial chamber descend steeply, the general trend was for the inclines to become less acute in the tombs of the Nineteenth Dynasty and, later still, to slope only slightly in those of the Twentieth Dynasty. ◆

◄ Tuthmosis IV is welcomed into the Afterlife by (from left) Hathor, Anubis and Osiris, in a scene typical of 18th Dynasty decoration of the well shaft and antechamber in royal tombs.

The Tomb of Amenhotep II

The tomb of Amenhotep II (c.1427–c.1400 BC) is one of the most interesting in the Valley of the Kings. Not only is the decoration of the burial chamber extremely beautiful, but the story of the discovery of the tomb and its contents is also intriguing.

The tomb was discovered in March 1898 by the French archaeologist Victor Loret, then head of the Egyptian Antiquities Service. The previous month he had discovered and cleared the tomb of Tuthmosis III (c.1479–c.1425 BC) high up in the cliffs of the Valley of the Kings, and it was while he was still engaged in this work that he made his next exciting find. He had set his workmen to explore another area in the Valley, where no tomb had yet been discovered. They noticed a large area of loose pieces of cut stone piled at the foot of the cliff. When they cleared this away, they found the top of a tomb entrance. Eventually, Loret was able to enter the steeply descending corridors and cross the well by means of a ladder. He found himself in a small two-pillared hall full of smashed pieces of funerary furniture, including three broken wooden boats. On closer inspection one bore a rather grisly cargo. Loret described his find thus:

I went forward with my candle and, horrible sight, a body lay there upon the boat, all black and hideous, its grimacing face turning towards me and looking at me, its long brown hair in sparse bunches around its head.

Loret had a fertile imagination, and in the heat of the moment he was convinced that he had found a human sacrifice or, at the very least, a tomb robber polished off during a fight over the division of the loot, or by the police interrupting the robbery. In fact, it turned out to be most likely that the body was that of Webensennu, the king's son, who in his lifetime had been in

▲ *The cartouche-shaped red sandstone coffin of Amenhotep II stands in a recess in his burial chamber. Isis and Nepthys guard his feet and head.*

charge of the royal chariot horses. This is suggested by the find in the same room of a *shabti*-figure (or model servant) inscribed with his name.

The burial chamber

As Loret entered the burial chamber, he saw six square pillars decorated on each face with images of Amenhotep II, identified by the accompanying cartouches, in the embrace of the deities Anubis, Hathor and Osiris. In the sunken area at the end of the burial chamber there was a sarcophagus. Loret could

scarcely contain his excitement as he went to examine it:

The sarcophagus was open, but was it empty? I did not dare to hope for the contrary as royal burials had never been found in the necropolis of the Valley, all of them having been moved in antiquity to a safe place. I reached the sarcophagus with difficulty being careful not to break anything underfoot. I could partially read the cartouches of Amenhotep II. I leant over the edge, bringing the light a little nearer. Victory! A dark coffin lay at the bottom, having at its head a bunch of flowers and at its feet a wreath of leaves...

Later, Loret was able to get a closer look at the coffin. To his relief the body was still inside, and was intact. 'It carried around the neck a garland of leaves and flowers, on the breast a little bouquet of mimosa, which hid the prenomen of Amenhotep II written on the sheet, the name which I later read.'

Apart from the mummy of Tutankhamun, that of Amenhotep II is the only one to have been found lying in his own tomb, albeit in what appears to have been a replacement coffin. Unlike the mummy of Tutankhamun, which still remains in his tomb, Amenhotep's was taken to the Cairo Museum later.

This was not the only surprise. Loret went on to clear the rooms that lay to the side of the burial chamber. The two left-hand ones were filled with storage jars, embalmed provisions, *shabti*-figures and other funerary goods. But on the right he found more mummies. The first chamber on the right contained a woman, a youth and a man. The second contained a further nine mummies, and turned out to be a cache of royal bodies removed from their tombs for safekeeping (see *The Fate of the Royal Mummies*). ◆

▼ *The starry ceiling of Amenhotep II's burial chamber is supported by six square pillars decorated with images of the king welcomed into the Afterlife by Anubis, Osiris and, shown below, Hathor, Mistress of the West. The figures are drawn in outline with only some decorative elements, such as Hathor's headdress and the panel surround, coloured in.*

The journey of the sun god

The walls of Amenhotep II's burial chamber are decorated with a complete version of the Am Duat, or 'Book of What is in the Underworld'. This text describes the king's nocturnal journey with the sun god through the Underworld and his rejuvenation as the sun rises next day.

The work is divided into 12 'chapters', which represent the 12 hours of the night. Vertical borders define these, and each is divided into three horizontal registers. The middle one shows the King and the sun god sailing through the Underworld and overcoming the many hazards of the journey. Finally, the king's mummy is shown propped against the wall as his spirit soars to paradise. The ceiling is painted blue with golden stars.

The Tomb of Seti I

The tomb of Seti I (c.1294–c.1279 BC) is the longest and deepest royal tomb in the Valley of the Kings. Its decoration is also the most complete, although there are some unfinished scenes. The basic plan is of the 'jogged-axis' type, but here it is complicated by the addition of several extra chambers.

Original features

From the entrance, the three usual corridors lead to a well shaft and a pillared hall. Then a new feature appears in the form of a second chamber, designed perhaps to fool tomb robbers. The burial chamber also has additional pillared rooms and ritual niches. A further innovation is a passage leading down from the burial chamber in the main part of the tomb to another pit deeper down, near the level of the water table. This may have had some symbolic significance, linking the burial chamber to the primordial waters and uniting the concepts of creation and re-creation. In a similar way, the Osireion of Seti's temple at Abydos, built in honour of Osiris, is also sunk deep in the ground so that at times it would be surrounded by water, like the primeval mound.

Tomb paintings

Another similarity with the Abydos temple is the quality of the decoration in the tomb. Most of it is embellished with beautiful figures of the king and the gods, in painted raised relief.

Seti's choice of themes sets a precedent for all the later tombs in the Valley. For the first time, the first two corridors are decorated with texts from the Litany of Re, which praises the sun god under 75 different names. Scenes from the Am Duat are also present in the second corridor, whereas in earlier tombs these appeared only in the burial chamber. The

▲ Ceilings of the burial chamber are decorated with deities and stars. Below are funerary texts to aid the king on his journey to the Afterlife.

well is decorated with images of the king before the gods, as in some earlier tombs. However, the pillared hall has scenes and texts from the Book of Gates and, again for the first time, an Osiris shrine marking the entrance to the lower part of the tomb. This style was followed in many later tombs. Seti's burial chamber is decorated with the earliest example of an astronomical ceiling, showing some of the constellations and a calendar with the 36 'decans', or groups of stars, into which the night sky was divided by the ancient Egyptians.

◄ Part of the astronomical ceiling in the burial chamber of Seti I showing the constellations.

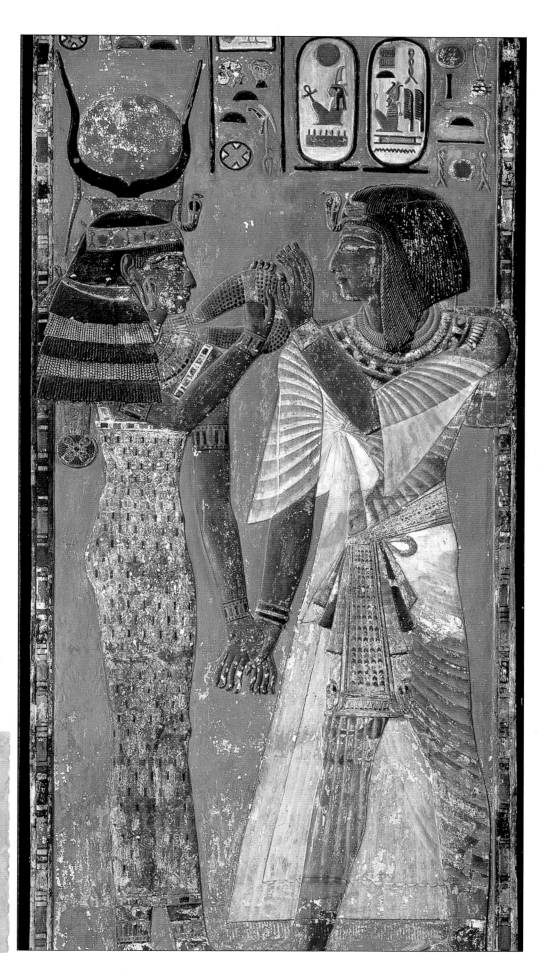

▶ *One of the masterpieces of ancient Egyptian art, this shows the goddess Hathor welcoming Seti I into the Afterlife.*

The mummy of Seti I

Giovanni Belzoni discovered the tomb in 1817. His most significant find at the site was the beautiful translucent calcite sarcophagus, also decorated with scenes and texts from the Book of Gates, now in Sir John Soane's Museum in London.

When Belzoni found the sarcophagus, it was empty. However, the mummy was found many years later by Emile Brugsch in the cache at Deir el-Bahri (see *The Fate of the Royal Mummies*). The body was quite well preserved, although the head had been detached from the body during one of several rewrappings by the high priests of Amun during the Twenty-first Dynasty (c.1069–c.945 BC). Inscriptions on the coffin, also restored by the priests, record Seti's removal from his own tomb in Year 10 of the reign of Siamun (c.978–c.959 BC), his reburial three days later in the tomb of Queen Inhapi, and his subsequent transfer to the cache in the reign of Sheshonq I (c.945–c.924 BC). There it remained until 1881 when it was removed with the other royal mummies to Cairo, where it is now on display in the Egyptian Museum. The tomb itself has been closed for restoration since 1991. ◆

The Book of Gates

This collection of magical spells, which decorated the pillared hall of Seti's tomb and his sarcophagus, was intended to enable the king to overcome the demons and powers of the Underworld. The spells provided him with the passwords he needed to get through the gates guarded by snakes and deities as he proceeded on his journey.

The Discovery of Tutankhamun's Tomb

Between 1903 and 1912, an American businessman, Theodore M. Davis, financed a series of excavations in the Valley of the Kings. One of those working for him was the experienced Egyptologist, Howard Carter (1874–1939). Together they made several important discoveries, including the (albeit robbed) tombs of Tuthmosis IV (c.1400–c.1390 BC) and Hatshepsut (c.1473–c.1458 BC), and the intact tomb of Yuya and Tuya, who may have been the great-grandparents of Tutankhamun (c.1336–c.1327 BC).

Davis also found various clues suggesting that the tomb of Tutankhamun might be in the vicinity. One was a robbers' cache containing items of Tutankhamun's funerary furniture. Another was a pit, discovered in 1907, containing seal impressions of Tutankhamun, linen bags filled with natron and other embalming materials, and the remains of his funerary feast. Finally, under a nearby boulder, Davis found a blue faience cup bearing the name of Tutankhamun. However, after several years of fruitless searching, Davis left the Valley convinced there were no more royal tombs to be found.

Howard Carter and his British patron, the fifth Earl of Carnarvon, gained the concession to dig and were ready to start work in 1914, but had to abandon the idea when World War I broke out. They started again in 1917, but had no more

▶ *Tutankhamun fulfils his traditional role as Horus harpooning the evil Seth.*

▲ *Discovered in the antechamber of the tomb, this magnificent box shows Tutankhamun charging into battle against his enemies.*

luck than Davis. After five unsuccessful seasons Lord Carnarvon was ready to give up, but Carter pleaded for just one more chance. Digging was resumed on 1 November 1921, the first job being to record and remove some ancient workmen's huts apparently used during the preparation of the tomb of Ramesses VI (c.1143–c.1136 BC). As they took down the old building, the top of a flight of steps was revealed.

Opening the tomb

By the next afternoon the stairway had been cleared and a doorway, fastened with the seal of the necropolis inspectors, had been found.

The next morning Carter sent a telegram to Lord Carnarvon, announcing his discovery. Lord Carnarvon and his daughter reached Luxor on 23 November. The staircase was again uncovered and the remaining four steps were cleared, revealing the lower part of the doorway. Much to the delight of the excavators, this was stamped with the seals of Tutankhamun, proving that his long-sought tomb was found. The king's seals were on part of the original blocking of the tomb, while those of the necropolis inspectors referred to a resealing, which implied that the tomb might still contain some funerary equipment.

After entering and clearing the sloping tunnel behind the door, they came to another sealed doorway. Carter described the mounting excitement:

Slowly, desperately slowly, it seemed to us as we watched, the remains of the passage debris that encumbered the lower part of the doorway were removed, until at last, the whole door was clear before us. The decisive moment had come. With trembling hands I made a tiny breach in the upper left-hand corner. Darkness and blank space as far as I could reach, showing that whatever lay beyond was empty and not filled like the passage we had just cleared.

Candle tests were then applied as a precaution against foul gasses, and then, widening the hole a little, I inserted a candle and peered in, Lord Carnarvon, Lady Evelyn and Callender standing anxiously nearby to hear the verdict. At first I could see nothing, the hot air escaping from the chamber causing the candle to flicker, but as my eyes grew accustomed to the gloom, details of the room within emerged slowly from the mist, strange statues and animals and gold, everywhere the glint of gold. For the moment, an eternity it must have seemed to those standing by, I was struck dumb with amazement, and when Lord Carnarvon, unable to stand the suspense any longer, inquired anxiously, 'Can you see anything?'

it was all I could do to get out the words, 'Yes. Wonderful things!' Then making the hole a little wider we inserted an electric torch.

Finds from the tomb

A painted wooden head of Tutankhamun emerging from a lotus flower was found among the rubble blocking the passage to the tomb. It shows Tutankhamun appearing as the sun god did at the time of creation from a lotus floating on the waters of the primordial ocean. It combines the idea of creation with the king's re-creation.

Three beds were found in the antechamber. One is in the form of a lion, representing the goddess Mehet, associated with Hathor, Sekhmet and Isis. Mehet is the deity responsible for the Nile flood. Another takes the form of a composite deity, part crocodile, part lion and part hippopotamus. She is Ammut, Devourer of the Dead. She stands near the scales in the Judgement Hall and devours anyone who fails to pass the test. The cow goddess depicted on the third bed is Mehet Weret or 'Great Flood'. She represents the primordial cow who rose from Nun, the primordial ocean, and bore the sun god Re, to the sky. She will raise Tutankhamun, too, so that he can join the sun god.

Tutankhamun's mummy was found in a gold coffin. It had been placed inside two more coffins, one inside the other. The innermost was made of gold and the second was of gilded wood covered with precious stones. These are on display in the Cairo Museum, along

▲ Tutankhamun and his wife, Ankehsenamun, depicted on the back of a gilded wooden throne, which is decorated with glass paste and semi-precious stones.

with the other treasures from the tomb. The body of Tutankhamun, now placed in the outermost coffin, still lies in his tomb in the Valley of the Kings.

Directly over the mummy's face was a solid gold mask. Tutankhamun is shown wearing the royal headdress, in which the blue stripes are made of glass paste in imitation of lapis lazuli. His eyes are inlaid with quartz and obsidian to make them sparkle and to emphasize that he is a living king. He wears a curved false beard to show that he has become Osiris.

The mummy of Tutankhamun was decorated with 150 pieces of jewellery, all of which are full of symbolism. The winged scarab is the sun god Khepri. He holds the lotus and papyrus, symbols of Upper and Lower Egypt, and *shen*-rings, symbols of eternity. At either side is the *uraeus*, the cobra that spits at Egypt's enemies, wearing a solar disc. Above is the solar boat carrying the *udjat*, or Eye of Horus (the moon). It is flanked by two more *uraei*, wearing moon discs. At the very top is the disc of the moon inside the lunar crescent. On the disc, Tutankhamun is crowned by Thoth and Re-Horakhty. The whole piece symbolizes the king's ascent to heaven and his rule throughout eternity. ◆

◄ The solid gold mask of Tuthankhamun was placed over the face of the mummy.

Texts from the Tomb of Ramesses VI

The tomb of Ramesses VI (c.1143–c.1136 BC) is a good example of the 'straight-axis' tomb plan. The floors of the first corridors slope only gently before descending to the lower passages and burial chamber. Inscriptions in the tomb state that it was prepared initially for Ramesses V (c.1147–c.1143 BC). There is no sign of Ramesses VI having usurped the tomb, so it is possible that both kings were buried here. Neither of their mummies was discovered in the tomb: both were found in the cache at Deir el-Bahri.

The choice of texts used for the decoration of this tomb is rather different from earlier ones, with a greater emphasis on the sun god Re and on astronomical texts. Unlike most tombs from the time of Seti I (c.1294–1279 BC), however, the Litany of Re does not appear, and is replaced by excerpts from the Book of Gates and the Book of Caverns. Apart from the text inscribed on the sarcophagus of Seti I, the most complete version of the Book of Gates appears in this tomb. The Book of Caverns is particularly concerned with rewards and punishments in the Afterlife, and especially with the annihilation of Re's enemies.

▲ The magnificent tomb of Ramesses VI is one of the largest and most complete in the Valley of the Kings. The walls are covered with collections of spells to effect the king's resurrection.

The first three corridors have astronomical ceilings and there are excerpts from the Books of the Heavens in the well room and first pillared hall. These books are a collection of texts that describe the sun's journey across the sky. They include the Book of the Day, the Book of the Night and the Book of the Divine Cow. Further extracts from these books decorate the ceilings of the lower passages and antechamber.

The walls of the corridors are painted with parts of the Am Duat or 'Book of What is in the Underworld', while the antechamber is decorated with images of the gods and sections of the Book of

◄ The scenes from the Book of the Earth show the rebirth of the sun, which symbolizes the resurrection of the King.

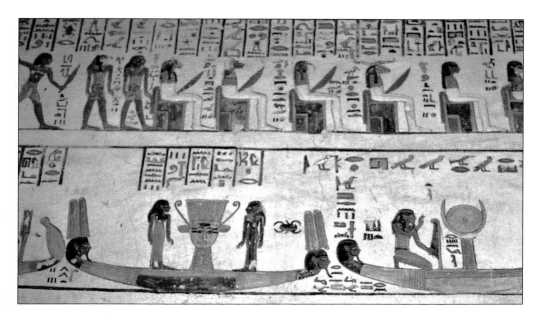

▶ *Boats in the retinue of the sun god accompany him though the Underworld. Above are avenging deities armed with knives to overcome Re's enemies.*

the Dead. This material is usually found inscribed on papyrus rolls in the tombs of commoners from the beginning of the New Kingdom (c.1550 BC). It is a collection of spells derived from the Middle Kingdom Coffin Texts and ultimately from the Old Kingdom Pyramid Texts, which were used exclusively in royal burials.

The magnificent ceiling of the burial chamber of Ramesses VI combines images of the sun god in the solar barque with the passage of the sun through the body of the sky goddess Nut.

The content of the texts

The funerary texts that decorate the walls of the royal tombs in the Valley of the Kings describe the voyage of the sun god, with whom the king is identified, through the Underworld. They enable the king to enter the Afterlife unmolested by the enemies of Re.

The earliest is the Am Duat. It tells of the sun god's journey through the 12 divisions of the Underworld, which are equated with the 12 hours of the night. Complete copies are found in the tombs of Tuthmosis III (c.1479– c.1425 BC) and Amenhotep II (c.1427– c.1400 BC). Portions decorate the walls of the lower passages of the tomb of Ramesses VI.

Nearer to the entrance are extracts from the Book of Gates, which also describes the sun god's journey through the hours of the night. The name of the book refers to the 12 gates through which the sun god passed and that divide one hour from another. One section of the Book of Gates depicts the Judgement Hall of Osiris where the hearts of the dead are weighed in the balance. The good are justified and wrongdoers condemned.

The Book of Caverns appears in the first three passages, the well room and the first pillared hall along with scenes from the Book of Gates. Osiris figures prominently in these texts where the sun god Re comes for him and punishes his enemies, condemning them to non-existence. In the pillared hall, Osiris wears a solar disc, which identifies him with Re so that they appear to be two aspects of one god. Elsewhere in the tomb, the sky goddess Nut carries the sun god on her hands. He is seen both as the disc of the sun and in human form with a ram's head. Four crocodiles on Nut's left are Re's enemies. On her right is the sun god in different forms.

The Books of the Heavens and a double image of the goddess Nut span the burial chamber. Here, the sun is shown as a disc being swallowed by the sky goddess and passing through her body to be reborn the next morning, and also as a ram-headed god sailing in the solar boat across the sky during the day. The king aspires to accompany the sun god through the Underworld, then to rise and sail with him upon the celestial waters throughout eternity. ◆

▼ *Depicted on the ceiling of the tomb, Nut swallows the sun in the evening whereupon it travels through her body during the night and is reborn at sunrise.*

The Fate of the Royal Mummies

In 1881, in the absence of Gaston Maspero, the then head of the Egyptian Antiquities Service, his assistant Emile Brugsch arrived in Luxor to investigate rumours concerning the discovery of a hitherto unknown tomb. For the previous ten years or so, objects such as funerary papyri, *shabtis* and canopic jars had been mysteriously appearing on the antiquities market from an undisclosed source. Brugsch's arrival in Luxor had, in fact, been prompted by the confession of the head of the Rassul family from Gurna on the West Bank, who claimed that members of his family had been responsible for removing these artefacts from a tomb in the cliffs at Deir el-Bahri.

The cache of Deir el-Bahri

How the tomb came to be discovered in the first place is not known, although several romantic stories are told about it. Some members of the Rassul family acted as guides for visiting travellers, and it may be that their intimate knowledge of the area led them to it. The family had certainly been suspected of untoward dealings in antiques, and two of them had been interrogated and tortured by the local mudir, or governor, Daud Pasha. In spite of some brutal treatment they refused to give anything away and it was only in the face of great family opposition that the headman, Muhammad Ahmed Abd el-Rassul, decided to go to the authorities.

Although Brugsch realized that there would be more than one royal mummy in the tomb, he was astounded by the number that met his eyes when he entered the first chamber. In a further chamber, he found even more mummies. In his haste to clear the tomb before local treasure hunters could lay their hands on the contents, however, no proper records were kept.

An Egyptian film made in 1969, *The Night of the Counting of Years*, is based on the story of the discovery of the cache. In one of its most moving scenes, the procession of donkeys and mules bearing their precious burdens reaches the Nile and the royal mummies are put on a boat. Women from the villages come down to the river to wail in mourning for the long-dead kings as they sail downstream to Cairo.

On his return to Egypt, Maspero paid a visit to Luxor to see the tomb for himself, and was soon able to recognize two different groups of mummies. Those from the further chamber were carefully wrapped and placed in distinctive coffins, with their funerary goods around them. These were the mummies of a family of high priests of Amun descended from Herihor, who ruled the Theban area from the end of the Twentieth Dynasty (c.1069 BC). The mummies of the other group proved to be of kings, queens and officials previously buried elsewhere. They included Ahmose, Amenhotep I, Tuthmosis II, Tuthmosis III, Ramesses I, Seti I, Ramesses II and Ramesses III.

On examining the notes written on the mummy wrappings, Maspero discovered that many of the royal mummies had had a somewhat eventful career. The notes revealed that some of the mummies had been restored and rewrapped several times, and moved from one hiding place to another over a period of about 70 years. During this time several mummies had been taken to the tomb of Seti I and restored there before being moved again. The tomb of Queen Inhapi is mentioned many times in these notes, and at one time it was believed that the tomb in which the cache was found was hers. Recent research has shown that her tomb was yet another halfway house, and that the final hiding place was in fact the family tomb of Pinedjem II, High Priest of Amun. The family burials in the end chamber were orderly and intact, whereas the royal mummies seemed to have been pushed into the first chamber rather unceremoniously, Queen Inhapi's among them, suggesting haste.

Royal mummies in the tomb of Amenhotep II

A second cache of nine royal mummies was found in a side chamber in the burial suite of Amenhotep II (c.1427–c.1400 BC) (see *The Tomb of Amenhotep II*). At first, Victor Loret, who discovered the tomb in 1898, thought they must be members of Amenhotep's family. He changed his mind when he examined them more closely:

▶ *The mummy of Ramesses II demonstrates the skill of the embalmer and the degree to which the technique of mummification had been perfected.*

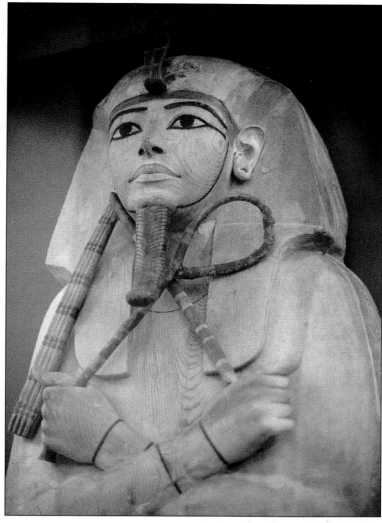

▲ *The lid of the coffin of Queen Maatkare, which was found in Deir el-Bahri. The daughter of the High Priest, she was installed as 'God's Wife of Amun', an important religious and political post.*

▲ *This wooden coffin, which housed the mummy of Ramesses II, found in the Deir el-Bahri cache, was possibly originally intended for Ramesses I.*

The coffins and mummies were a uniform grey colour. I leaned over the nearest coffin and blew on it so as to read the name. The grey tint was a layer of dust which flew away and allowed me to read the nomen and prenomen of Ramesses IV. Was I in a cache of royal coffins? I blew away the dust from a second coffin and a cartouche revealed itself, illegible for an instant, painted in matte black on a shiny black ground. I went over to the other coffins – everywhere cartouches.

He realized that he had indeed discovered a cache of royal mummies. The names of the kings proved to be every bit as illustrious as those in the tomb at Deir el-Bahri: Tuthmosis IV, Amenhotep III, Merenptah, Seti II, Siptah, Ramesses IV, Ramesses V, Ramesses VI and an unnamed female, perhaps Tawosret, wife of Seti II.

It is now thought that these mummies, and the various pieces of funerary equipment that were found with them, had been collected from other tombs and caches at the same time as the body of Amenhotep II himself had been rewrapped, since all the bodies bore a similar type of docket. This must have been some time after Year 12 of the Twenty-first Dynasty king Smendes (c.1069–c.1043 BC) because a note on the mummy wrappings of Amenhotep III states that the mummy had been restored that year in his own tomb.

Some of the mummies were in the 'wrong' coffins. Amenhotep III was in a coffin inscribed with the name of Ramesses III, while the lid had originally belonged to Seti II. Merenptah lay in the lower part of a coffin inscribed for Sethnakhte, while the female mummy was lying on the upturned lid.

Is there a third cache?

Not all the bodies of the kings of the New Kingdom have yet been found. The missing mummies include those of Tuthmosis I, Akhenaten, Horemheb, Ay and Hatshepsut. An inscription found by Sir Alan Gardiner at the entrance to the tomb of Horemheb may refer to the restoration of further royal mummies. This is supported by the fact that Theodore Davis found many dismembered skeletons, as well as funeral garlands of a type dating from the Third Intermediate Period (c.1069–c.747 BC), when he was working in the Valley of the Kings in 1908. ◆

The Craftsmen's Village at Deir el-Medina

The craftsmen who lived in the village known to the ancient Egyptians as the Place of Truth, now Deir el-Medina, were highly skilled sculptors and artists who worked on the royal tombs in the Valley of the Kings. Their village is one of the most interesting sites of ancient Egypt for two reasons: not only have very few other occupation sites been discovered but large amounts of written material, often inscribed on limestone chippings called 'ostraca', were found during excavation.

The village was laid out around a main street with side alleys leading from it. It originally consisted of 70 houses, and about 40 more were added during the Nineteenth Dynasty (c.1295–c.1186 BC). The houses were built of rough field stones and mudbrick, and consisted of four or five rooms: an entrance, a main room, two smaller rooms behind that and a kitchen with a cellar. A staircase led to the roof. The windows were high up on the walls, allowing light to enter while excluding the full glare of the sun. A feature of the main room was a mudbrick platform approached by a short flight of steps, which may have functioned either as a shrine or as a birthing bed. The village was about 3km (2 miles) away from the Nile Valley,

apparently for security reasons. Bricks stamped with the name of Tuthmosis I (c.1504–c.1492 BC) suggest that the village was founded in his reign.

The craftsmen left the village at the close of the Twentieth Dynasty (c.1069 BC), as from that time the kings were buried in the Delta.

Organization of the workers

The workmen were divided into two gangs, called, like a ship's crew, the gang

▲ *The interior decoration of the tomb of Pashedu, who was one of the highly skilled craftsmen who lived in the village.*

of the right and the gang of the left. Most lived permanently in the village, although the numbers varied according to the amount of work to be done. New workers were recruited from among the sons of the craftsmen. There were two foremen, one for each gang, who were appointed in the first place by the vizier on behalf of the king. Thereafter the position remained in the family unless something untoward happened, when a new appointment would be made. As well as being in charge of work on the tomb, the two foremen controlled the village and its activities.

Next in importance came the scribe of the tomb. His chief duty was to keep a register of work done and to note absentees. He also recorded the

◀ *The view from the surrounding hills of the village of Deir el-Medina, which housed Egypt's best artisans from the 18th to 20th Dynasties.*

◀ *Anherkhau and his wife depicted in his tomb at Deir el-Medina, where he was foreman.*

distribution of tools, materials and wages. The deputy foremen, usually the sons or near relatives of the foremen, sometimes undertook the supervision and distribution of supplies, while the guardians of the tomb controlled the royal storehouses where the tools and materials were kept. They were aided by doorkeepers, who worked in shifts to guard the entrances to the royal tombs, and the *medjay*, who were stationed outside the village. It was their job to preserve law and order and prevent unauthorized entry to the tombs in the Valley of the Kings.

The villagers were supported by the 'servants of the tomb', who lived outside the village but were sent by the central administration to supply the inhabitants with firewood, water, fish and vegetables. Some were potters and washermen. There were also slaves who ground flour for the villagers. All payment was in kind, and these goods formed part of the wages of the craftsmen. The workers also received monthly rations of emmer wheat and barley, as well as irregular payments of dates, cakes and beer. On special occasions, there were bonus payments of blocks of salt, natron (a salt used in the mummification process) and meat.

Generally, the rations seem to have been more than adequate, and there was usually something over that could be used for barter or even bribes. However, the payment was not always prompt and delays could mean hardship. When their wages did not materialize in Year 29 of Ramesses III (c.1184–c.1153 BC), the workers went on strike and demonstrated in front of the Ramesseum. The 'police' seem to have been sympathetic and arranged for them to be supplied with food to tide them over until they were paid. There were more strikes later in the year and in subsequent reigns.

The working week consisted of eight days, with rest days on the ninth and tenth, so the workers had six days off a month, although they seem to have taken longer 'weekends' quite frequently. They also had holidays on religious festivals. During the week, they may have camped-out near the Valley of the Kings. Otherwise they lived with their wives and children in the village.

Village life

On their days off, the villagers might set to work on their own and each other's tombs. The workmen who excavated and decorated the royal tombs were the best craftsmen of ancient Egypt. They included stonemasons, draughtsmen, sculptors, artists and carpenters. They trained their sons and passed on their skills to them. Consequently, their own tombs are some of the most beautiful on the West Bank.

Those who had other skills did a brisk trade in coffins and funeral equipment.

Otherwise, their leisure time seems to have been spent reading, committing adultery or taking each other to court.

Local justice

The village had its own court, composed of the foremen and deputies, the scribe and some of the craftsmen. It is not known when it met, but it was a source of great entertainment. The village court had the authority to deal with all civil action and minor criminal matters. (Major crime was dealt with by the vizier's court at Thebes.) Most of the cases concerned non-payment for goods or services rendered, and were fairly trivial matters. The villagers conducted their own cases, so there were no fees to be paid to lawyers and arguments often dragged on for years. The craftsman Menna, for example, sued the chief of police over non-payment for a pot of fat and certain articles of clothing. The case lasted for 11 years. ◆

The register

The record of attendance kept by the scribe of the tomb shows that many of the craftsmen had days off due to illness. Scorpion stings and eye diseases are often mentioned. Some had time off for family reasons, often to do with funeral arrangements. Other much less reputable reasons were also noted: one man had had a row with his wife and another had been out drinking with his friend Khons and was in no fit state to work the next morning.

Tomb Robbery

The fact that most of the royal mummies were removed from their tombs in the Valley of the Kings and hidden elsewhere suggests that they had been in danger of violation by tomb robbers. There is also clear evidence of a break-in at the tomb of Tutankhamun.

Tomb robbery papyri

A great deal is known about the activities of tomb robbers, and the measures taken to deal with them, from a collection of papyri dating from the end of the Twentieth Dynasty (c.1069 BC). At this time there seems to have been a general breakdown in law and order, and the robbing of tombs was a symptom of these troubled times. The papyri contain the names of the tombs that had been robbed, the confessions of the robbers, and the results of the official inspections of the tombs undertaken in answer to allegations of theft. The discovery of the true extent of the tomb robbing was complicated by the rivalry of the two mayors of Thebes. Puwero, the mayor of West Thebes, was also chief of the necropolis police and particularly resented the implication that he had not been doing his job properly. Eventually, his resistance was broken down and the investigations began. A commission of high officials was set up to look into the reports of robberies in the necropolis and to inspect the tombs for damage.

Apart from the document now known as Papyrus Mayer B, which records the robbery of the tomb of Ramesses VI (c.1143–c.1136 BC), the papyri all refer to the plundering of tombs outside the Valley of the Kings. The royal tombs in question were situated at the nearby necropolis of Dra Abu el-Naga, where the kings of the Seventeenth Dynasty (c.1650–c.1550 BC) were buried. The

▼ *The robbery of the tomb of Ramasses VI was documented in antiquity in Papyrus Mayer B. The entrance to his tomb can be seen below centre.*

commission extracted some extraordinary confessions from the accused, such as this one recorded in Papyrus Leopold-Amherst from the stonemason Amenpanufer in Year 16 of the reign of Ramesses IX (c.1126–c.1108 BC):

We went in accordance with our regular habit, and we found the pyramid of King Sobekemsef, this being not at all like the pyramids and tombs of the nobles which we habitually went to rob. We took our copper tools and we broke into the pyramid of this king through its innermost part. We found its underground chambers and we took lighted candles in our hands and we went down. Then we broke through the rubble that we found at the mouth of the recess, and found this god lying at the back of his burial place. And we found the burial place of Queen Nubkhaas, his queen, situated beside him, it being

▲ A papyrus records the confession of robbers who entered the tombs of kings and commoners alike and stripped the mummies of their jewellery.

protected and guarded by plaster and covered with rubble. This we also broke through, and found her there, resting in similar fashion. We opened their sarcophagi and their coffins in which they were, and found the noble mummy of this king equipped with a falchion; a large number of amulets and jewels of gold were upon his neck, and his headpiece of gold was upon him. The noble mummy of this king was completely bedecked with gold, and his coffins were adorned with gold and silver, inside and out and inlaid with all sorts of precious stones. We collected the gold we found on the mummy of this god, together with that on his amulets and the jewels which were upon his neck, and that on the coffin in which he was resting, and we found the queen in exactly the same state. We collected all that we found upon her likewise and set fire to their coffins. We took their furniture which we found with them consisting of articles of gold, silver and bronze, and divided it among ourselves. And we made into eight parts the gold which we found on these two gods coming from their mummies, amulets, jewels and their coffins, and 20 deben of gold fell to each of the eight of us, making 160 deben [14.5kg (32lb)], the fragments of furniture not being included. Then we crossed over to Thebes.

The confessions, from both men and women, were often extracted under torture. A certain Mutemwia, whose husband the measurer, Pawero, had been involved in robbing the tombs, was questioned concerning the whereabouts of the stolen goods, and denied all knowledge of them, but under torture 'with the birch and the screw' confessed that her husband had hidden his loot in the house of his brother-in-law.

The punishments meted out to the robbers are known from the oath that they were required to swear when they gave testimony: 'As Amun lives and as the ruler lives, if I be found to have had anything to do with any one of the thieves may I be mutilated in nose and ears and be placed on the stake.'

The tombs of priests and other commoners were not immune from violation by the robbers, who dragged the bodies out of their coffins to strip off their jewellery, and left them out in the desert. The commission also discovered that some of the workmen from Deir el-Medina were involved. Eight of the craftsmen were arrested, including the two deputy foremen. The stolen goods were found in their homes, and various members of other settlements on the west bank were named as receivers of stolen goods. A further investigation led to a complete purge of the village hierarchy, and new foremen and deputies were appointed. ◆

Queens, Princes and Officials

The pharaohs were not the only people to be buried in the Valley of the Kings. Other members of the royal family were buried there too. Tuthmosis III (c.1479–c.1425 BC) prepared a splendid tomb close to his own for his chief wife, Hatshepsut-Merytre, while Isisnofret, the wife of Merenptah (c.1213–c.1203 BC) was buried with him in his tomb in the Valley of the Kings. Royal sons buried in the Valley include the sons of Ramesses II (c.1279–c.1213 BC). Commoners of high rank could also be buried there, the most famous being Yuya and Tuya, the parents of Queen Tiye, and the chancellor Bay, who took charge in the unsettled period at the end of the Nineteenth Dynasty (c.1295–c.1186 BC).

Amenhotep III (c.1390–c.1352 BC) prepared places for two of his wives, Tiye and Sitamun, within his own tomb in the Western Valley. In the Ramesside Period, however, royal wives were usually buried in the nearby necropolis of the Valley of the Queens, although some of the royal children had been buried there since early in the Eighteenth Dynasty (c.1550–c.1295 BC). The most appealing of these tombs is that of Nefertari, Great Royal Wife of Ramesses II, and of the sons of Ramesses III (c.1184–c.1153 BC), Khaemwese and Amun-hir-khopshef. Most of the officials of the Ramesside Period are buried in beautifully decorated tombs in or near the modern village of Gurna.

◀ *This wall painting from the tomb of Nefertari in the Valley of the Queens shows the queen, identified in the cartouche, wearing the vulture headdress, which links her with Isis and Hathor.*

The Tomb of Nefertari

Nefertari was the favourite wife of Ramesses II (c.1279–c.1213 BC), the first of eight that he married during his long reign of 67 years. His other wives included two of his own daughters, his sister and two Hittite princesses. Nefertari seems to have belonged to a high-ranking family, but was not herself royal because she is never given the title of 'King's Daughter'. It is thought that she probably came from Thebes because she is always called 'Beloved of Mut', and Mut was an important goddess in the Theban area. Although she was given the title 'Mother of the King' and had several sons, they all seem to have died before their father. Merenptah (c.1213–c.1203 BC), the next king, was the son of Istnofret, Ramesses II's other chief queen.

Nefertari seems to have played a prominent ceremonial role on state and religious occasions. In the first year of Ramesses' reign she officiated at the investiture ceremony of Nebwenenef as Chief Prophet of Amun at Abydos. She also appears in Year 3 on the New Pylon, a ceremonial gateway, which Ramesses II built at the Luxor Temple, and in diminutive form among the royal statues with which he embellished the forecourt. Ramesses honoured her most of all at Abu Simbel in Nubia. He built two temples there, one for Re-Horakhty and the other state deities, including himself, and the other dedicated to the goddess Hathor and Nefertari.

Tomb paintings

Nefertari's tomb in the Valley of the Queens is the most beautiful of all the royal tombs. It is an absolute feast for the eyes, the bright colours used for the figures being enhanced by the white background and the dark blue of the ceiling. It was discovered in 1904 by Ernesto Schiaparelli, and was closed to the public shortly afterwards because the painted plaster was in such a fragile condition. It has recently been conserved by the Getty Conservation Institute and is now open to the public again for the first time in many years. However, the numbers of visitors to the tomb are strictly controlled, so that this treasure may be preserved for future generations.

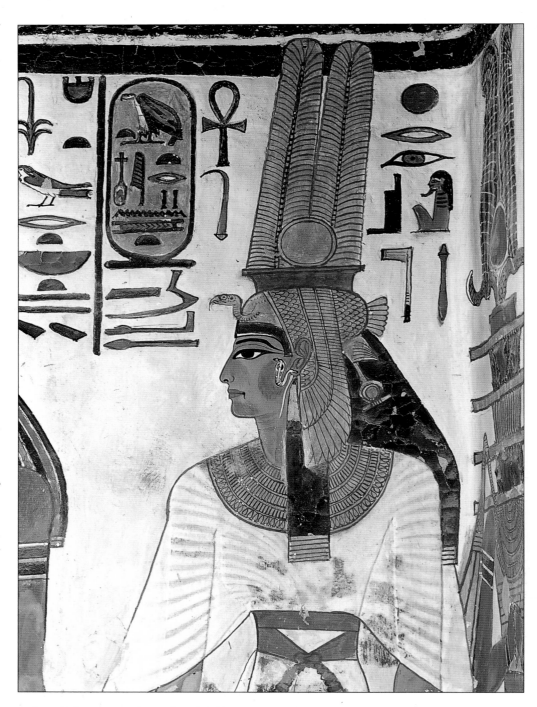

▲ *Nefertari, the favourite wife of Ramesses II, is introduced to various deities in scenes from the vestibule of her tomb in the Valley of the Queens.*

Much of the decoration concerns the Heliopolitan creation myth, according to which Atum, the sun god, emerged from the primordial ocean to create Shu,

▶ *Wearing a diaphanous gown of fine linen and the vulture headdress, Nefertari plays* senet, *a board game similar to chess or draughts.*

the god of air, and Tefnut, the goddess of moisture, from his bodily fluid, which contained both male and female elements necessary for creation. Their union produced Geb, the earth god, and Nut, the sky goddess, who also married and produced Isis, Osiris, Seth and Nephthys. Linked to this is the myth of Osiris, in which he, as the highly esteemed king of Egypt, was murdered by his jealous brother Seth. After he had been restored to life he entered the Underworld to become the judge of the dead while his son, Horus, avenged his death to become the next king of Egypt. The upper section of the west wall of Chamber C shows Isis and Nephthys as kites at the foot and head of the dead Osiris. In the myth they beat the air with their wings to enable Osiris to breathe again and

▼ *The elegantly dressed Nefertari offers two nu-pots to Hathor; from the southern wall alongside the steps leading to the burial chamber.*

so be restored to life. Nefertari hopes to be restored in the same way.

Here, as in several later tombs in the Valley of the Kings, the sun god is assimilated with Osiris. On the west wall of Chamber G, Isis and Nephthys are depicted on each side of a god who takes the form of a mummy, as Osiris did, and is represented with the ram's head of the sun god. The text on the left

reads, 'It is Osiris who sets as Re,' and on the right, 'It is Re who sets as Osiris.' Osiris and the sun god Re appear in various forms throughout the tomb, and Nefertari associates herself with both.

Elsewhere in the tomb, deities lead Nefertari into the presence of the gods. In Recess E, Hathor, the cow goddess, who was often depicted as the mother of the king, conducts Nefertari on her way through the Afterlife. She is also shown welcoming her on one of the pillars of Chamber K. ◆

Conservation

The Getty Conservation Institute has cleaned the walls of the salt crystals that had formed over the centuries, and stabilized the plaster. It is adamant that the tomb has not been subjected to 'restoration', by which it means the addition of missing colour. No new paint was added – what can be seen is the original work. Where the original decoration has disappeared, blank patches of plaster, made from local materials, now cover the gaps.

The Tomb of Ay

Ay (c.1327–c.1323 BC) was an army commander who became king of Egypt after the death of Tutankhamun (c.1336–c.1327 BC). He may have been related to the royal family by marriage: there is evidence to suggest that he was the brother of Queen Tiye, wife of Amenhotep III (c.1390–c.1352 BC), while it is also sometimes mooted that he may have been the father of Nefertiti, the wife of Akhenaten (c.1352–c.1336 BC). He is shown on the walls of the burial chamber in the tomb of Tutankhamun, officiating at the young king's funeral, and thus staking his claim to the throne.

Whatever the truth about his relationship to the royal family, it is clear that Ay was a high official at the court of Akhenaten, where he held the title 'Superintendent of the Royal Horses'. Later, he rose to power as vizier and royal chancellor. Not unnaturally, he began work on a large and splendid tomb at Akhenaten's capital Akhetaten (Tell el-Amarna). This was left unfinished but is famous for its inscription of an extended version of the Hymn to the Aten, in praise of the sun disc, which was worshipped exclusively during Akhenaten's reign.

The Western Valley tomb

The tomb that was prepared for Ay as king lies in the wild and rugged Western Valley. Ay had a comparatively short reign of four or five years, and it appears that the tomb may previously have been intended for somebody else. Candidates include Tutankhamun or even Tuthmosis, the elder brother of Akhenaten who died before his father, Amenhotep III, who is also buried in the Western Valley. In any event, the decoration of the tomb is very similar in many ways to that of Tutankhamun's. It was discovered by Giovanni Belzoni in 1816 but was not fully excavated until 1972, when it was cleared by Otto Schaden.

The architecture of Ay's tomb is akin to that of the royal tomb at Tell el-Amarna, having a straight axis but with the burial chamber slightly to one side. A new feature is the slots cut into the walls of the first corridor, to accommodate a beam that was used to lower the sarcophagus into the tomb.

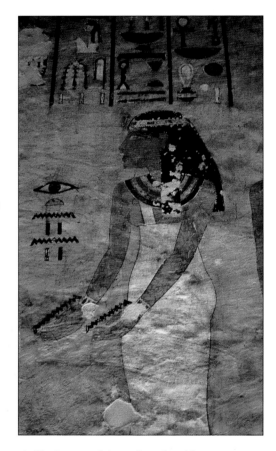

▲ *The images of the gods and goddesses were left untouched. Here, the goddess Nut offers Ay the sign for water so he will not die of thirst on his journey to the Afterlife.*

Tomb decoration

The artistic style and the motifs of the tomb decoration so resemble those of Tutankhamun that it would seem that the same artist was responsible for both. In both tombs there are scenes showing the deceased king and his *ka*, or vital essence, being welcomed into the Underworld by Osiris and Hathor. Another scene shows 12 baboons, who represent the 12 hours of the night, while a further scene shows the boat of the sun god in his scarab beetle form, preceded by five deities.

A unique feature for this period is the scene of fishing and fowling in the marshes, in which Ay is shown hunting with his wife. This is a theme more usually found in the tombs of nobles,

◄ *Ay was considered to be the last king of the Amarna period and consequently his tomb was badly mutilated. All images of Ay have been hacked away.*

although a similar scene appears in the much earlier mortuary temple of the Fifth Dynasty king Sahure (c.2487–c.2475 BC) at Abusir. There may even be another parallel with the tomb of Tutankhamun: although hunting is not part of the painted decoration there, it is perhaps reflected in the hunting scene on the small gilded shrine found among the grave goods. It is also echoed in two statuettes of Tutankhamun on a papyrus skiff, with a harpoon poised to thrust into his prey in the water.

A small room leading from the burial chamber is the canopic chamber, where the internal organs of the king would have been preserved. The entrance has been decorated with two pairs of figures who are sometimes identified with the Four Sons of Horus, the guardian deities of the viscera.

The images of Ay himself, although not those of his *ka*, were destroyed in antiquity, presumably because of his association with the heretical regime of Akhenaten. This probably happened

▲ *Ay performing the Opening of the Mouth ceremony in the tomb of Tutankhamun. Usually this is done by the son of the deceased. As Tutankhamun had no son, this scene indicates Ay as his successor.*

in the early Ramesseside Period, when steps were taken to obliterate the memory of Akhenaten from history. Ay's sarcophagus, also similar to that of Tutankhamun, was found in fragments, although it has now been restored. His mummy has never been found. ◆

The Tomb of Yuya and Tuya

Yuya and Tuya were the parents of Queen Tiye, the wife of Amenhotep III (c.1390–c.1352 BC). Because of their close connection with the king, they were allowed the honour of having a tomb in the Valley of the Kings, even though they themselves were not royal. They were very important people in their own right, however. Yuya was in charge of the king's chariotry and Tuya was 'Chief Lady of the Harem'. Yuya was also called 'God's Father', a reference to his relationship to the king.

The tomb of Yuya and Tuya was discovered in 1905 by James Quibell, and was found to contain the most spectacular collection of funerary goods that had yet come to light in the Valley of the Kings. This came as a complete surprise to the excavators, as it was obvious that the tomb had been broken into in antiquity. It had been resealed with a stone wall covered in mud plaster and stamped with the necropolis seal, and there was evidence to suggest that this had happened more than once.

The robbers had gone through the tomb feverishly searching for valuables. The mummy bandages had been ripped apart and the lids of boxes torn off in their haste. However, as was the case with the tomb of Tutankhamun, it appears that the robbers were disturbed just in time. A chariot yoke, a gilded wooden staff and a heart scarab had been abandoned in the corridor as they fled. Nevertheless, the robbers seem to have made away with all the smaller valuables. There was no jewellery in the tomb apart from that found on the mummies themselves. Other costly items such as oils and perfumes were also missing. The many treasures that remained are now in the Cairo Museum.

Quibell was working in the Valley under the auspices of Theodore Davis, who cleared the tomb in great haste while Quibell was away. Unfortunately, as time was at a premium, he did not take the trouble to record the finds properly, particularly their position in the tomb. It is not known whether Yuya or Tuya died first, and such information might have helped to answer that unsolved question.

The mummies

The mummified bodies of Yuya and Tuya were found within the tomb. Although they had been partly un-wrapped, they were very well preserved and are two of the finest examples known. Quibell wrote that

▲ *Tuya's jewel casket of gilded wood inlaid with elements made of ebony, pink-stained ivory and blue faience. The upper part is decorated with cartouches of Amenhotep III, her son-in-law.*

Yuya's features were perfectly preserved, so that 'The powerful and dignified face of the old man strikes one as something human, as a face one would recognize in a portrait.' Yuya's mummy was placed in a nest of four coffins, one rectangular (but bottomless) and three anthropoid. Of these, the enormous outer one was covered in bitumen and bound with inscribed bands of gilt; the next had similar bands over a background of silver leaf; and the innermost was gilded all over and inlaid with glass hieroglyphs in imitation of jewels.

The faces of both mummies had been covered with masks. Royal mummy masks were usually made of beaten gold, but those of Yuya and Tuya were of gilded cartonnage (linen stiffened with plaster). Yuya's mask had been broken into fragments. That of Tuya was broken in two, but has now been restored. The

▼ *The goddess Isis protects the mummy just as she protected Osiris in mythology.*

▲ *Gilded wooden side panels from a chair with images of the protector deities, Bes and Taweret.*

mask had been covered with a piece of very fine linen. When this was removed it revealed a beautiful portrait of Tuya. She has a charming smile and her eyes have been inlaid with blue glass and quartz, to which red touches have been added in order to give her a lifelike appearance. Her eyebrows have been inlaid and her eyes outlined with glass in imitation of lapis lazuli. She wears a long striated wig that is kept in place with a floral headband. Covering the upper part of her body is a huge collar composed of rows of leaf and petal shapes inlaid into a background of coloured glass, which imitates bands of lapis lazuli, turquoise and carnelian.

The four canopic jars of Tuya are particularly interesting. Each contains one of her internal organs wrapped up in a little mummiform parcel, and each miniature 'mummy' has been given its own small mummy mask.

The grave goods

The tomb was packed with all sorts of funerary goods, including several pieces of furniture, one of which was a beautiful jewel casket that had belonged to Tuya. It is made of gilded wood in the form of a little shrine and is inlaid with ebony, rose-tinted ivory and blue faience. The box is decorated with the cartouches of Amenhotep III, her son-in-law, and her daughter, Queen Tiye. A frieze running around the lower part of the casket is composed of the hieroglyphs for 'life' and 'prosperity', thus wishing the owner a blissful Afterlife.

Three beautiful chairs were also found in the tomb, one of which had belonged to Sitamun, the daughter of Amenhotep III and granddaughter of Tuya and Yuya. It is made of dark red wood and decorated with side panels covered in gold leaf. These show figures of the god Bes, protector of families and helper of women in childbirth, wielding knives and beating on drums to drive away evil spirits. The panel on the chairback shows Sitamun being presented with golden collars by Syrian princesses. There were also three beds whose headboards were decorated with images of Bes.

Yuya took his chariot with him to the tomb. It is made of gilded wood and is in remarkably good condition, being almost complete. It is decorated with spirals and rosettes in gilded plaster. Measures were also taken to ensure that Yuya and Tuya did not go hungry. Some of the boxes found in the tomb contained dried meat, geese and ducks to sustain them throughout eternity. ◆

▼ *The funerary mask of Yuya, father of Queen Tiye. His mummy is one of the best preserved ever found.*

▼ *The gilded plaster mask that once covered the head of the mummy of Tuya, mother of Queen Tiye.*

A royal seat

The Empress Eugénie, wife of Napoleon III of France, visited the tomb while Quibell was finishing its clearance. When he apologized for the fact that all the (modern) chairs had been packed away and there was nowhere to sit, the eye of the empress lit upon the chair of Sitamun and she decided that it would suit her very well. The archaeologists held their breaths as she sat down, but fortunately for both empress and chair it stood up to the strain.

The Tomb of the Sons of Ramesses II

Ramesses II (c.1279–c.1213 BC) had an extremely long reign of 67 years, and must have been over 90 years old when he died. He had several wives and concubines, and fathered a great number of children, many of whom he outlived. His successor, Merenptah (c.1213–c.1203 BC), whose own tomb is in the Valley of the Kings, was his thirteenth son, his older brothers having died before their father. Although they never inherited the throne, these brothers seem to have been given the privilege of burial in the Valley of the Kings (apart from Khaemwese, who may be buried near Memphis, where he was High Priest of Ptah). Other sons of Ramesses II may well have been buried there too.

Only 70m (77yd) from the tomb of Tutankhamun and almost opposite the tomb of Ramesses II, Dr Kent Weeks, an American archaeologist and director of the Theban Mapping Project, discovered an enormous enigmatic structure hailed by many as the most exciting archaeological discovery of modern times. It is thought to be the burial place of the sons of Ramesses II.

New discoveries

The existence of this tomb, known as KV5, has long been known, and it was partially explored as long ago as 1825 by the English Egyptologist James Burton. Howard Carter also examined the area around the tomb in 1902, but was not able to penetrate beyond the entrance. Kent Weeks and his team from the American University in Cairo relocated the tomb in 1985–6. As the first two chambers were cleared of debris it became obvious that a great deal of damage had been caused by the tourist coaches using the road above the tomb, and by a broken sewer. After the first season of work on the tomb, Weeks realized that the structure he had found was unique. He went so far as to claim

that it was the tomb of at least two, and perhaps as many as eleven of Ramesses' sons. However, since then, many more chambers have been discovered. In May 1995 Kent Weeks made an exciting announcement:

▲ *The names of many of Ramesses II's sons are known from inscriptions elsewhere, such as this relief from the Temple of Luxor. They include Meryatum (his sixteenth son) and Seti (shown here), who both died in their twenties as did several of their brothers.*

Last February, excavating through the flood-borne debris that fills the tomb, my staff and I found a passageway leading past 20 chambers to a statue of the god Osiris. Two transverse corridors, each with another 20 chambers, extend beyond that. At the end of the corridors there are stairs and sloping corridors apparently leading to even more rooms on a lower level. The tomb could be the largest ever found in Egypt.

There are likely to be about 150 chambers and corridors in the complex, of which fewer than seven per cent have yet been cleared. In fact, Weeks has no intention of trying to complete the excavation himself. He wants to leave parts of the building to be explored by future generations, using new excavation techniques as they are developed. In the meantime, he and his team will concentrate on making the structure safe and recording, conserving and studying the wall decorations, inscriptions and artefacts that have already been discovered.

Tomb layout and decoration

The plan of the complex as a whole is unique, although there are some individual features that are similar to other tombs in the Valley. Some Eighteenth Dynasty tombs have a narrow entrance that leads directly into a chamber, rather than the more usual passage, while some of the chambers have vaulted ceilings like tombs of the Nineteenth Dynasty. In this tomb there are two chambers, which give way to a large pillared hall. Leading from the hall is a huge T-shaped area lined

with many alcoves or small chambers. In the centre of the bar of the T is a statue of Osiris and, at each end, a stairway descends to a lower level where two passages slope, in the opposite direction to the upper level, towards the tomb of Ramesses II.

That this unique structure was intended as the burial place of Ramesses II's sons is indicated in the decoration of the first two chambers, where there are painted reliefs showing the king leading his sons into the presence of the funerary deities. These were originally similar to the scenes in the tomb of Amun-hir-khopshef (see *Tombs of the Sons of Ramesses III*), in the Valley of the Queens, but so much damage had been done by floodwater and sewage that the painted plaster had come adrift and lay in fragments among the debris. However, it has been possible, with the help of a skilled conservator, to preserve the south-western corner of the tomb. There, the name, titles and figure of another Amun-hir-khopshef, Ramesses II's eldest son, came to light. He is shown with his father, who introduces him to the goddess Hathor and the funerary deity Sokar.

Another son was 'discovered' on the south wall. He was named Ramesses after his father, who is shown leading him into the presence of Nefertem, the god of the lotus blossom. The name of a further son, Seti, was found on a fragment of a canopic jar in the

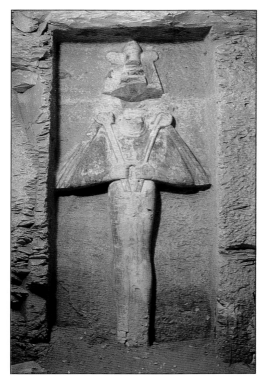

▲ *This rock-cut figure of Osiris, King and Judge of the Dead, was found in his shrine in the T-shaped tomb of the sons of Ramesses II.*

second chamber, and a fourth, Meryatum, on an ostracon found by Howard Carter. The names of a total of 52 sons of Ramesses II are known from other sources. It will be interesting to see how many eventually come to light in this tomb. The images of several more sons appear in the painted decoration of the tomb, but the inscriptions accompanying them have unfortunately been destroyed. Several skulls and a whole skeleton have been found, but there is, as yet, no clear evidence for their identification.

Another puzzle is that the entrances to the side chambers of the T-shaped section are too small to accommodate sarcophagi, so what was the purpose of these chambers? It is known that the main doorways of the tomb were widened at some time, as the alterations have cut into figures and texts already carved on the walls. This would have made it possible to bring sarcophagi inside the tomb itself. Perhaps they were then placed in parts as yet unexplored. ◆

◀ *Inscribed* shabtis *were found among the funerary equipment.*

The Tombs of the Sons of Ramesses III

Of the five tombs prepared by Ramesses III (c.1184–c.1153 BC) for his sons, three were found by Ernesto Schiaparelli in the early 1900s. The most beautiful are those of Amun-hir-khopshef and Khaemwese, both of which were commissioned in Year 28, towards the end of the reign of Ramesses III. The tombs are decorated in painted carved relief.

Little is known of these two princes and nothing at all about the circumstances of their deaths, although the sequence in which the tombs were prepared can be worked out from developments in their decoration. Even the names of the princes are something of a mystery as they do not match up with a list of 13 sons in Ramesses III's mortuary temple at Medinet Habu. It is sometimes suggested that the princes suffered from some kind of congenital disease that led to an early death, and for this reason Ramesses made provision for them during his later years. Or were they perhaps carried off by some kind of epidemic? The ages of the princes are also uncertain. They are represented with the distinctive hairstyle known as the 'sidelock of youth', which suggests that they were very young, although it may simply indicate that they were sons. However, the fact that their father accompanies them into the Underworld and introduces them to the funerary deities seems to confirm their youth.

An unusual feature of these tombs is that it is the king, and not a god or goddess, who introduces his sons to the various deities. The main theme of the decoration in each tomb is that of the prince undertaking a ritual journey. Eventually, he finds himself alone in the Afterlife, which is symbolized by the tomb. By using the correct 'passwords' from the Book of the Dead he is able to proceed through the gates of the Underworld and join Osiris in paradise. Finally, he is reborn and becomes one of the 'imperishable stars'.   ◆

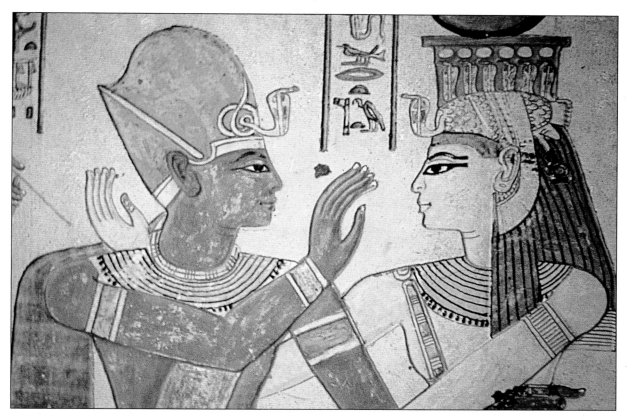

◄ *Amun-hir-khopshef is depicted wearing the 'side-lock of youth' to show he is the son of Ramesses III; from his tomb in the Valley of the Queens.*

▲ *Ramesses III is received by Hathor, in her roles as Mistress of the West and as one of the main funerary goddesses.*

▼ *Ramesses III introduces his son Amun-hir-khopshef to the deities of the Underworld. The age at which he died is uncertain.*

The Tomb of Rekhmire

The vizier was the king's chief minister and the most important official in the land, and Rekhmire held this position under Tuthmosis III (c.1479–c.1425 BC) and Amenhotep II (c.1427–c.1400 BC). His tomb is one of the most attractive and informative of all the tombs of the New Kingdom (c.1550–c.1069 BC). It is located in the modern village of Gurna near the Valley of the Kings, the burial place of the rulers Rekhmire served during his lifetime.

Plan of the tomb

The tomb is cut into the rock and follows the usual plan of officials' tombs of this period. The doorway leads into an oblong chamber, with a long corridor leading from the centre of the back wall, opposite the entrance. The texts that form part of the wall decoration in this tomb are particularly interesting. They describe Rekhmire's installation as vizier and the wide-ranging nature of his work. As well as holding a number of priestly offices, he was also in charge of every government department and was also chief judge. His installation as vizier would have been the climax of an illustrious career.

One intriguing fact about this tomb is that there is no burial shaft, so it would seem that Rekhmire was eventually buried elsewhere. It is possible, as he was such an important person, that he was buried in the Valley of the Kings, although this is not known for certain.

The role of the vizier

The procedure followed in the court of the vizier is described in some of the texts inscribed on the tomb walls. The vizier sat on a chair wearing a cape and his chain of office, with an animal skin behind his back and another at his feet. He had his staff close by and 40 leather rods set out in front of him.

▼ *As vizier, part of Rekhmire's duties was to supervise activities in the state workshops. These carpenters are working on a fine chest.*

Other senior officials and his scribes also sat with him in the court.

The vizier's other duties included reporting daily to the king about all the comings and goings in and out of the palace. He had to inform the king about the income and expenditure of the royal estates, the government finances and the border fortifications. He appointed officials and saw that the local governors were aware of the king's commands, and that they sent in their reports as required. The army was mobilized and the system of compulsory state labour (the corvée) was organized by the vizier, who also conducted land surveys, fixed local boundaries and fitted out ships. He was responsible for law and order, as well as reporting on the height of the Nile and the rise of Sirius, the Dog Star, the appearance of which heralded the Egyptian New Year.

The tomb's painted decoration includes many scenes depicting all sorts of agricultural operations and craft

▼ Dancers and musicians entertaining guests at a funerary feast is a common theme depicted on the tomb walls of this period.

work. Farmworkers, sculptors, brickmakers and jewellers mingle on the tomb walls. The oblong hall has registers of gifts and shows tribute bearers from Nubia, Syria and Crete. They are all recognizable from the faithful depiction of the physical characteristics of the various ethnic groups and by the objects and animals they bring to the vizier. Other scenes show emissaries from the different regions of Egypt coming to present their taxes, while elsewhere in the tomb there are depictions of funerary and ritual scenes. ◆

▲ A scene from a jeweller's workshop shows gold being melted in the fire, possibly to be worked into a fine gold collar.

The ship of state

During his long career, Rekhmire was close to the king. He served him well and helped him steer the ship of state, while as a judge he felt his conduct was impeccable:

I was the heart of the Lord, the ears and eyes of my Sovereign. I was his skipper, and knew not slumber by night or by day. Whether I stood or sat, my heart was set upon prow rope and stern rope, and the sounding pole was never idle in my hands... I judged rich and poor alike. I rescued the weak from the strong... I defended the widow. I established the son and heir on the seat of his father... I judged great matters... I caused both parties to go away satisfied. I did not pervert the course of justice for reward. I was not deaf to the empty-handed. I did not accept anyone's bribe...

The Tombs of Eighteenth Dynasty Officials

The ancient Egyptians believed that the Afterlife would be very much like life on earth. They painted scenes on the walls of their tomb chapels recreating their current life to perpetuate it for eternity, and these scenes tell us a great deal about everyday life in ancient Egypt.

The tomb of Nakht

Although it is very tiny, the tomb of Nakht is one of the most charming in the Theban necropolis. Nakht was 'Chief of the Granaries', 'Keeper of the King's Vineyards' and 'Royal Astronomer' under Tuthmosis IV (c.1400–c.1390 BC). Both Nakht and his wife, Tawi, who was a chantress of Amun, were buried here.

On the left of the entrance to Nakht's tomb there are several scenes depicting life on an estate. Two farmworkers are planting seeds, while others plough with wooden ox-drawn ploughs. Farther along are scenes of harvesting, where the corn is cut with sickles and flax is pulled out by the roots. In the next section, the workers use wooden blades to scoop up the threshed grain to separate the grain from the chaff. Meanwhile, Nakht sits in his booth and oversees the work.

Opposite the agricultural scenes is a depiction of a funerary banquet. This is one of the most famous scenes in ancient Egyptian art. The guests are seated on elegant chairs and have cones of scented ointment on their heads. Young girls present bead collars to the ladies, who are dressed in glamorous diaphanous dresses and wear complicated wigs and enormous gold earrings. Musicians playing the harp, lute and some kind of flute entertain the guests. Under a chair, a cat is hastily devouring a stolen piece of fish.

To the right of the door, Nakht and his wife sit in front of an offering table. A similar scene is almost opposite. On the left side of the chapel is a false door,

which supplies details of Nakht's life and implies that he hopes to enjoy this same rank and status in the next life. At the bottom, Hathor, goddess of the west, welcomes him into the Afterlife.

Just beyond there is a scene in which Nakht is fishing and fowling in the marshes with his wife and son. Nakht is shown twice, almost as a mirror image of himself, on a skiff in the papyrus marshes. To the left he is aiming a throwing-stick at a flock of birds, while to the right he is about to harpoon a fish.

Further along are two scenes showing the preparation of food and drink. In the top register, the workers are picking large bunches of grapes in the vineyard. Others are trampling the grapes, while another man catches the grape juice in jars and sets them up on a shelf to let the wine ferment. Below, a net is spread to catch birds. When the net is full, a cord is pulled tight and the birds are trapped. The sequel shows the birds being plucked and hung in preparation for cooking.

▲ *Part of a scene from the tomb of Nakht shows him catching wildfowl in the marshes. The other 'half' is a mirror image, which shows him fishing.*

▼ *These musicians, playing a harp, a lute and a double flute, entertain guests at a funeral banquet; from the tomb of Nakht.*

The tomb of Menna

Menna was 'Scribe of the Fields of the Lords of the Two Lands of Upper and Lower Egypt' during the reign of Tuthmosis IV. Not surprisingly, a whole wall of his tomb chapel is devoted to agricultural scenes. The top register shows officials measuring the land and assessing the crop. Other sections depict the harvesters reaping in the fields. The grain is carried off to the granary in huge baskets. Scribes, perched on great heaps of grain, record the amounts harvested under the eagle eye of Menna himself, whose status is emphasized by the rather smart horse and chariot waiting to convey him to Thebes. Although such scenes were common to many tomb chapels of this period, the artist has included many details that make it an individual work. A mother is nursing her baby under a tree and two girls are quarrelling. Another vignette shows a girl taking a thorn out of her friend's foot.

The usual scene of hunting in the marshes is also included in this tomb. Like Nakht, Menna is shown in a papyrus boat with his wife and children. He is catching two fish and is about to hurl his throwing-stick in the direction of a papyrus thicket, which is full of nesting birds and small animals.

▶ *Sennefer sails upstream from Abydos having completed his pilgrimage to the shrine of Osiris.*

▲ *Sennefer, overseer of the gardens of the god Amun, and his wife in his Theban tomb, which is decorated with a trailing vine.*

A different scene shows Menna on a voyage to Abydos, possibly recording a pilgrimage he made to the tomb of Osiris. However, below this are scenes showing the rites performed on the mummy before burial, so it is equally likely that the upper scene is connected with Menna's funeral. In the opposite corner at the far end of the chapel is a painting showing the ritual of the Weighing of the Heart.

The tomb of Sennefer

Sennefer was Mayor of Thebes and 'Overseer of the Granaries and Gardens of Amun' during the reign of Amenhotep II (c.1427–c.1400 BC). Judging from the decoration of his tomb chapel, he may also have been the king's chief vintner. One of the most delightful aspects of the tomb is the vine that is painted growing up the chapel wall and trailing across the ceiling. The surface of the ceiling is rough and the artist has made ingenious use of any raised areas by transforming them into bunches of grapes.

The wall paintings are equally charming. In the antechamber, Sennefer is brought offerings by his daughter and priests. Other scenes show Sennefer and his wife, Meryt, worshipping Osiris. In the main chamber, they are depicted entering the Underworld, sitting side by side on elegantly carved chairs, and accepting offerings. In one of the most attractive scenes, Sennefer is seated in front of an offering table holding to his nose a lotus flower (the symbol of re-creation). His wife sits at his feet, affectionately clasping his leg. ◆

Index

Abusir, necropolis at 40–1, 56
Abusir Papyri 41
Abydos: excavations at 26–7
    mastaba tombs 30–1
Afterlife 34
    Book of Caverns 102
    capital city for 74
    of the king 38–9, 62, 80–1
    reflection of life on earth 124
    and renewal of royal power (*heb sed*)
      75, 78–9
    ritual journey to 120
    servants for (*shabtis*) 46, 47, 96
    and voyage of the sun god 34, 62,
      80–1, 103
agricultural scenes 81, 84, 124, 125
Akerblad, Johan David 16–17
Akhenaten 78, 79, 87, 114, 115
Akhetaten (Tell el-Amarna) 20,
    26, 114
Alexander the Great 10
Alexandria 10, 11, 71
Am Duat 98, 102, 103
Amélineau, Emile Clément 26, 30, 31
Amenemhat III 20, 42, 44, 45
Amenhotep I 104
Amenhotep II, 96–7, 122
    royal mummies in 104
Amenhotep III 11, 15, 79, 92, 111, 114
Amenhotep IV *see* Akhenaten
Ammut, Devourer of the Dead 101
Amun-hir-khopshef 111, 120, 121
antiquities, race for 18–19
Anubis 97
Apis bulls: *heb sed* festival 72, 78, 79
    Serapaeum (burial place) 22, 23,
      88–9
artisans, tombs of 68
astronomical ceilings 98–9, 102
Aten 79
Atum, sun god 112
Augustus 11
Ay, tomb of 92, 114–15

Barsanti, Alessandro 81
Bastet, cat-goddess 79
Belzoni, Giovanni 19, 54, 99, 114
Beni Hasan, tombs at 20

Bent Pyramid 34–5
Bes, goddess of families and
    childbirth 117
bird tomb of Neferherenptah 84
boats: of Khufu 62–3
    pits 50, 53, 62
    solar 62
    wood for 63
Book of Cairenes 103
Book of Caverns 102
Book of Gates 99, 102, 103
Book of the Dead 102, 120
Book of the Earth 102
'Book of What is in the Underworld'
    (Am Duat) 97, 98, 102, 103
Books of the Heavens 102, 103
Borschardt, Ludwig 40
Brugsch, Emile 99, 104
Brunton, Guy 44
Bruyère, Bernard 106
building methods, pyramids 36, 37, 58
Burckhardt, Jean-Louis 19
Burton, James 118

canopic vessels 44, 61, 117
Canopus Decree 21
Carnarvon, Lord 100–1
Carter, Howard 100–1, 118, 119
carved reliefs: pyramids 40–1, 53, 81
    tombs 86
cat goddess 79
catacombs 88–9

Cerny, Jaroslav 106
Champollion, Jean-François 16–17,
    18, 19
Cleopatra 16
Cleopatra's Needle 25
Colossi of Memnon 10, 11
conservation 113
Constantine 11
Copts 72
craftsmen: scenes of 65, 67, 81, 84,
    85, 123
    village of Deir el-Medina 106–7

Dahshur, pyramids of 34–5
Darius I 89
Davis, Theodore M. 100, 116
de Sacy, Sylvestre 16
Deir el-Bahri 104
Deir el-Medina, craftsmen's village
    106–7
Delta sites 26
*Denkmäler aus Aegypten und
    Aethiopien* 21
Denon, Baron Dominique Vivant 15
Description de l'Egypte 14, 15
Djedkare 40
Djer, tomb of 31
Djoser: *ka* statues of 75, 76
    Step Pyramid of 32–3, 72, 73,
      74–7, 78
Dream Stela 55
Drovetti, Bernadino 18, 19

dwarfs 85
    cemetery 69
    tombs of 49

Early Dynastic Period 29
    mastabas 30–1, 32
Edwards, Amelia 24–5, 81, 89
Egypt Exploration Society (Egypt
    Exploration Fund) 25, 72, 86
Egyptologists 20–1, 22–3, 26–7
Egyptomania, in Europe 15, 18
Eighteenth Dynasty 94, 95, 118
    officials' tombs 124–5
el-Lahun (agricultural centre) 42
Emery, Walter B. 31
Eugénie, Empress 117

Faiyum, pyramids of 26
false doors 67, 69
ferryman, mythical 38
Fifth Dynasty 40–1
First Dynasty 20, 27, 62
First Intermediate Period 32
Firth, Sir Charles 81
fishing scenes 83, 84, 85, 115, 124
Fourth Dynasty 49
French Commission on Arts and
    Sciences 14
furniture 60–1, 117

Geb, earth god 113
Gebel Barkal 20
Getty Conservation Institute 112, 113
Giza, pyramids of 10, 13, 48–69
god, king as 91
Graeco-Roman Period 89
graffiti 11, 35, 76–7
Granite Temple 54
Great Pyramid, of Khufu 36, 50, 52–3,
    60, 64, 66–7

Hadrian 10, 11
hairstyles: 'sidelock of youth' 120
Hathor 97, 113, 121
    sexual love, goddess of 44, 57
Hatshepsut-Merytre 111
Hawass, Dr Zahi 53
heaven, prerogative of kings 39

heb sed (royal jubilee festival) 75, 76, 78–9
Heliopolitan creation myth 112–13
Hemen, falcon god 47
Hephaestus, temple of 72
Herodotus 9, 10, 36, 37, 43, 53, 72, 89
    on pyramids of Giza 58–9
Hetepheres 65
    tomb of 50, 60–1
hieroglyphs 16–17, 68, 81
Histories, The 10
Horemheb, tomb of 87, 95
horse burials 46–7
Horus 55, 57, 61, 101, 113
Huni 34
hunting scenes 115, 124, 125
Hymn to Aten 114

Idu, mastaba of 64, 67
Imhotep 32, 77
Inhapi 104
Isis 57, 71, 113
Istnofret 111
Iymery 67

Jeffreys, David 72
jewel casket, in tomb of Yuya and Tuya 116, 117
jewellery: royal 44–5
    workshop scene 123
jubilee festivals *see heb sed*

ka (spirit) 114
    statues 75, 76
Kagemni, mastaba of 85
Kahun, workers' town 43
Karnak, temples of 15, 18, 19, 20, 79
Khaemwese 80, 88, 89, 111, 118, 120
Khafre: diorite statues of 23, 55
    pyramid of 23, 26, 50, 54–5
Khasekhemwy 31
kheker frieze 33
Khufu 58
    boats of 62–3
    Great Pyramid of 35, 50, 52–3, 60
king, burial of 94–5
Kushite kings 46–7

labourers, tombs of 68
Labyrinth, the 20, 43
languages 16–17
Lauer, Jean-Philippe 74, 75, 79
Lepsius, Carl Richard 20–1, 86
Lettre à M. Dacier 17

Litany of Re 98, 102
Loret, Victor 96–7, 104–5
Luxor, Temple of, village beneath ruins of 24–5

Manners and Customs of the Ancient Egyptians, The 20
maps 12, 13, 14, 86
Mariette, Auguste 22–3, 25, 26, 54, 55, 88
Martin, Professor Geoffrey 21, 86
Maspero, Gaston 80, 104
mastabas 29, 50, 64, 68, 72
    Early Dynastic Period 30–1, 32
Maya, tomb of 21, 86–7
Mehet, deity 101
Meidum Pyramid 34
Memphis 22, 70–89
Menkaure 50, 56–7, 59
    reign of 59
Menna (Scribe of the Fields), tomb of 125
Merenptah 112, 118
Mereruka, mastaba of 73, 84–5
Meresankh III, tomb of 64–5
Middle Kingdom 42, 45, 72
Min 72
mortuary temples 35, 40, 53, 54, 57, 77, 81
    Labyrinth, the 43
    Valley of the Kings 94
    West Thebes 108
mummies 46, 69
    Apis bulls 88
    fate of royal 104–5
    lost evidence for 27
    Meresankh III 64
    Seti I 99
    tomb of Amenhotep II 97
    tomb of Nefer 83
    Yuya and Tuya 116–17
Mustufa, Ahmed Yussef 62
Mycerinus *see* Menkaure
mythology, in Pyramid Texts 38

Nakht, tomb of 124
Napoleon 14
Naqada 26, 27, 29
Narmer Palette 83
Nefer, tomb of 82–3
Neferirkare, pyramid of 41
Nefertari 111–13
Nefertiti 78, 79
Nekhbet, vulture goddess 45

Nephthys 71, 113
Netjerikhet *see* Djoser
New Kingdom 46, 72, 122
    tombs 86–7
    Valley of the Kings 91, 94
New Year, Egyptian 123
Nile River 9, 58, 63, 72
Nineteenth Dynasty 94, 95, 111, 119
Niuserre, sun temple of 41
Norden, Friderik 13
Nubkhaas 108
Nuri, burials at 47
Nut, sky goddess 38, 103, 113, 115

obelisks: Cleopatra's Needle 25
    hieroglyph inscriptions 11
Observations on Egypt 13
offerings chapels 65, 67
Old Kingdom 32, 34, 60
    religious belief 38
    tombs 64, 67, 82–5
Osiris: Apis bulls 88
    festival of 71, 97
    identified with Re 113
    rock-art figure of 118
    Underworld god 22, 113
Osorkon II 79

Palermo Stone 63
palm-log ceilings 32, 33
Paneb, notorious inhabitant of craftsmen's village 107
Papyrus Mayer B 108
passwords, to the Underworld 120
pectorals 44, 45, 101
Pepi I 39
Pepi II 38, 66
Petrie, Flinders 25, 26–7, 29, 31, 43, 44
Pharaonic Period 71
Piy 46
plant forms, in building 32–3
Pliny the Elder 11
Pococke, Richard 13, 88
Predynastic Period 29
    tombs of 31
prisoners, scenes of 86, 87
Ptah 71
    Apis bulls 88
    temple of 72
Ptolemaic Period 10, 71
Ptolemy V 16, 17
Ptolemy VIII 79
Pyramid Texts 32, 38–9, 62, 74, 80–1, 103

pyramids: complexes 28–47, 50, 53
    construction methods 36–7, 58
    design 52
    of Giza 10, 13, 49–69
    mudbrick 42–3
    step 32–3, 34
    'town' of Western Cemetery 66

Qar, mastaba of 64, 66
Quibell, James 116

Ra *see* Re
Ramesses II 17, 18, 72, 79, 88, 111, 112
    tomb of sons of 118–19
Ramesses III, tombs of sons of 119, 120–1
Ramesses IV, texts from tomb of 102–3
Rassul family 99
Re, sun god 38, 39, 80
    boats of 62, 63
    identified with Osiris 113
    voyage through the Underworld 79
Red Chapel, of Hatshepsut 79
Red Pyramid 34–5
reeds, in building 32–3
register of work 107
Reisner, George 57, 60, 65
Rekhmire, tomb of 122–3
Rosetta Stone 16–17, 21
royal burial ground (Valley of the Kings) 92–3

Sahure: mortuary temple of 115
    pyramid complex 40–1
Saite Period 77, 89
Salt, Henry 18

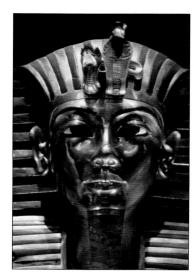

Saqqara, cemetery site 21, 22, 31, 72–3
Schaden, Otto 114
scripts 16–17
Sed-Festival *see heb sed*
Sekhmet, lion-headed goddess 19
Seneb, chief of the dwarfs 69
Sennefer, tomb of 125
Senusret II 44
    pyramid of 42, 44
Senusret III 45
sequence dating 27
Serapaeum 22, 72, 88–9
serdab (statue chamber) 75, 77, 85
Seth 71, 101, 103, 113
Seti I, tomb of 19, 98–9
Seti II 19
Seventeenth Dynasty 108
shabtis (servants for the Afterlife) 46,
    47, 96, 119
Shepseskaf 57
ship of state, steered by Rekhmire 123
Shu, god of air 38, 112
Sicard, Father Claude 12
silver mirror, of Princess
    Sithathoriunet 44
Sirius, the Dog Star 123
Sitamun, chair of 117
Sixth Dynasty 38
slaves 58
Sneferu 60, 63
    pyramids of 34–5
Sobekemsef, pyramid of 108
spells: Book of Gates 98, 99
    Book of the Dead 102
    Pyramid Texts 32, 38–9, 62, 74,
    80–1, 103
sphinxes 12, 14, 15, 22, 55
    symbol of royal power 54
statues: in mastabas of Qar and
    Idu 66
    in mastabas of workers' cemetery
    68–9
    in tomb of Mereruka 85
    in tomb of Queen Meresankh 65
    Tutankhamun 101
step pyramids 32–3, 34
stone, first architecture in 32–3
Strabo 10, 22, 88
sun god: Sphinx manifestation of 55
    Tutankhamun as 101
    voyage through Underworld 96, 103
sun temples 41, 56

Taharqo, pyramid of 47
Tefnut, goddess of moisture 113
temples, architecture 33

Teti 38, 39, 73
Theban Mapping Project 118
Thebes 91
Theodosius I 11
Thoth, god of wisdom 38
Thoth of Pnubs 208
Thousand Miles up the Nile, A 24–5
Tiye 111, 116
tomb layouts 94–5, 98, 102, 114,
    119, 122
tomb robberies 88–9, 108–9
Travels in Egypt and Nubia 13
Turin Canon 20
Tutankhamun 21, 86, 87, 92, 114
    tomb of 100–1, 108
Tuthmosis I 106
Tuthmosis II 92, 93
Tuthmosis III 11, 17, 111, 122
Twelfth Dynasty 44–5
Twentieth Dynasty 95, 108
Twenty-fifth Dynasty 46

Unas 38
    pyramid of 73, 80–1
Underworld 71
    Book of Gates 99
    Osiris 113
    Pyramid Texts 80
    ritual journey through 120
    Sokar and Osiris 22
    sun god's voyage through 96, 103
    tomb layouts 95
Userkaf, sun temple of 41

Valley of the Kings 9, 10, 12, 13, 14,
    20, 36, 46, 63, 90–109, 111, 116
Valley of the Queens 111, 112, 119
valley temples 53
    pyramid of Khafre 54–5
    pyramid of Menkaure 57
    Valley of the Kings 94
Vansleb, Father 12
vizier, role of 122–3
votive tablets 88–9
*Voyages dans la Basse et la Haute
    Egypte* 15
Vyse, Howard 56

Weeks, Dr Kent 118–19
Weighing of the Heart ritual 125
Wilkinson, John Gardner 20–1
Wilson, Sir Erasmus 25
workers, tombs of 68–9

Young, Dr Thomas 16, 17
Yuya and Tuya, tomb of 111, 116–17

Picture Credits

Sources of Quotes

The author and publishers would like to thank publishers for permission to quote from the following titles. Every effort has been made to identify sources and we apologize for any omissions:
Page 10: Austin, M M, *The Hellenistic World from Alexander to the Roman Conquest*, Cambridge, 1981
Page 15: Denon, V, *Travels in Upper and Lower Egypt*, London, 1802
Pages 22, 89: Vercoutter, J, *Search for Ancient Egypt*, London, 1992
Pages 24–5: Edwards, A, *A Thousand Miles Up the Nile*, London, 1877
Page 26: Petrie, W M F, *Seventy Years in Archaeology*, London, 1939
Pages 38–9, 80–1: Lichtheim, M, *Ancient Egyptian Literature*, Vols I–III, Berkeley, 1973, 1976, 1980
Pages 58–3, 88: Herodotus, *The Histories* (trans. Aubrey de Selincourt), London, 1954 Page 77: Lauer, J-P, *The Pyramids of Sakkara*, Paris, 1991
Pages 86–7: Martin, G T, *Hidden Tombs of Memphis*, London, 1991
Page 96: Romer, J, *Valley of the Kings*, London, 1881
Pages 100–1: Carter, H, *The Tomb of Tutankhamun*, London, 1923
Pages 108–9: Spencer, A J, *Death in Ancient Egypt*, London, 1982
Page 119: Weeks, K, *The Lost Tomb*, London, 1998